REPROBATION ASSERTED

by

JOHN BUNYAN

author of

Pilgrim's Progress
Holy War
Grace Abounding
Etc.

Reiner Publications
Swengel, Pa. 17880

1969

EDITOR'S ADVERTISEMENT.

This valuable tract was first published without a date, but according to Doe's List, about the year 1674, and has never been reprinted in a separate volume; it appeared in only one edition of the collected works of John Bunyan—that with the notes by Ryland and Mason; and in his select works, published in America in 1832. No man could have been better qualified to write upon the subject of reprobation than Bunyan.—His extraordinary knowledge of, and fervent attachment to, the holy oracles, peculiarly fitted him with unwavering verity to display this doctrine of divine truth. He was incapable of any misrepresentation with a view of concealing what fallen reason might deem a deformity, or to render the doctrines of the cross palatable to mankind. His object is to display the truth, and then humbly to submit to the wisdom of God, and zealously to vindicate it. There is no subject which more fully displays our fallen nature, than that of reprobation. All mankind agree in opinion, that there ever has been an elect, or good class of society; and a reprobate, or worthless and bad class; varying in turpitude or in goodness to a great extent and in almost imperceptible degrees. All must unite in ascribing to God that divine foreknowledge that renders ten thousand years but as one day, or hour, or moment in his sight. All ascribe to his omnipotence the power to ordain or decree what shall come to pass —and where is the spirit that can demonstrate a shade of difference between such foreknowledge and preordination. All agree that in the lower class of animals some of the same species pass their lives

in luxury and comfort, while others are cruelly tor-
mented, this world comprising their whole term of
existence; and will those who refuse to submit to
the sovereignty of God in the doctrine of election
dare to arraign his conduct in leaving some out of
his electing love?   The reprobate or worthless lose
nothing by the happiness of others.   It is inscrut-
ably hid from mankind who are the elect, until the
Holy Spirit influences them with the love of God
in Christ Jesus, and this sometimes in the last
moments of life.   There is every encouragement,
nay incentive, to the sinner who feels the burthen
of guilt to fly for refuge to the hope set before
him in the gospel.   'It *is* a faithful saying, and
worthy of all acceptation, that Christ Jesus came
into the world to save SINNERS;' even the chief of
sinners.   The glad tidings are addressed to ALL
sin-sick souls; and Bunyan's statement of this
truth is clear, scriptural, and reasonable.   Very
different is the account of reprobation given by R.
Resburie in his Stop to the Gangrene of Arminian-
ism, 1651.   'For the reprobate God decrees the
permitting of sin in order to hardening, and their
hardening in it, in order to their condemnation.'
p. 69.   'As election is the book of life, so reprobation of death; the names of the reprobate are there
registered for destruction.' p. 73.   It is much to
be regretted that sentiments like these have been
too commonly uttered.   It is as an antidote to such
ideas that this little work was written; but, unfor-
tunately, it has never been widely circulated and
read.   May the divine blessing follow this attempt
to spread these important, although to many, un-
palatable, doctrines.

GEORGE OFFOR.

JOHN BUNYAN

DISCOURSING TO THE TOWNS PEOPLE OF BEDFORD

"Accordingly when the people were assembled with no weapons but their Bibles.
the constable entered and arrested the preacher"

Life of Bunyan

REPROBATION ASSERTED.

THE CONTENTS OF THE CHAPTERS.

REPROBATION ASSERTED.

'What then? Israel hath not obtained that which he seeketh for; but the election hath obtained it, and the rest were blinded.'—Rom. xi. 7.

CHAP. I.

That there is a Reprobation.

IN my discourse upon this subject, I shall study as much brevity as clearness and edification will allow me; not adding words to make the volume swell, but contracting myself within the bounds of few lines, for the profit and commodity of those that shall take the pains to read my labours. And though I might abundantly multiply arguments for the evincing and vindicating this conclusion, yet I shall content myself with some few scripture demonstrations: the first of which I shall gather out of the ninth of the Romans, from that discourse of the apostle's, touching the children of the flesh, and the children of the promise.

1. At the beginning of this chapter, we find the apostle grievously lamenting and bemoaning of the Jews, at the consideration of their miserable state: 'I say the truth in Christ, (saith he) I lie not, my conscience also bearing me witness in the Holy Ghost, that I have great heaviness and continual sorrow in my heart. For I could wish that myself were accursed from Christ for my brethren, my kinsmen according to the flesh:' Poor hearts,

saith he, they will perish; they are a miserable sad and helpless people; their eyes are darkened that they may not see, and their back is bowed down alway. Ro. xi. 10. Wherefore? Have they not the means of grace? Yes verily, and that in goodly measure. First they 'are Israelites; to whom *pertaineth* the adoption, and the glory, and the covenants, and the giving of the law, and the service *of God*, and the promises; whose *are* the fathers, and of whom as concerning the flesh Christ *came*, who is over all, God blessed for ever. Amen.' What then should be the reason? Why saith he, though they be the children of Abraham according to the flesh, yet they are the children of Abraham BUT according to the flesh: 'For they *are* not all Israel (in the best sense) which are of Israel: neither, because they are the seed of Abraham, *are they* all children: but, in Isaac shall thy seed be called.' That is, they that are the children of the flesh, they are not the children of God; but the children of the promise shall be counted for the seed. So then, here you see that they that are only the children of the flesh, as the greatest part of Israel were, they are those that are neither counted for the seed, the children of promise, nor the children of God; but are rejected, and of the reprobation. This therefore shall at this time serve for the first scripture-demonstration.

2. Another scripture you have in the eleventh chapter of this epistle, from these words, 'The election hath obtained it, and the REST were blinded.' Ro. xi. 7. These words are shedding* words,

---

* 'Shedding words' means 'scattering or spreading words,' as in Acts ii. 33; now obsolete.—ED.

they sever between men and men; the election, the rest; the chosen, the left; the embraced, the refused: 'The election have obtained it, and the *rest* were blinded.' By *rest* here, must needs be understood those not elect, because set one in opposition to the other; and if not elect, what then but reprobate?

3. A third scripture is that in the Acts of the Apostles, 'And as many as were ordained to eternal life, believed.' xiii. 48. 'And as many;' by these words, as by the former, you may see how the Holy Ghost distinguisheth or divideth between men and men; the sons, and the sons of Adam. 'As many as were ordained to eternal life, believed:' If by *many* here, we are to understand every individual, then not only the whole world must at least believe the gospel, of which we see the most fall short, but they must be ordained to eternal life; which other scriptures contradict: for there is the rest, besides the elect; the stubble and chaff, as well as wheat: *many* therefore must here include but some; 'For though - Israel be as the sand of the sea, a remnant shall be saved.' Ro. ix. 27. Is. i. 9. and x. 22, 23.

I might here multiply many other texts, but in the mouth of two or three witnesses shall every word be established. Let these therefore for this, suffice to prove that there is a reprobation. For this I say, though the children of the flesh, the *rest* besides the election, and the like, were not mentioned in the word; yet seeing there is such a thing as the children of the promise, the seed, the children of God, and the like, and that too under several other phrases, as predestinated, foreknown, chosen in Christ, and written in the book of life, and appointed unto life, with many others: I say seeing these things are thus apparent, it is without doubt, that there is such a thing as a reprobation also. Ro. viii. Ep. i. 3, 4. 1 Th. v. 9.

Nay, further, From the very word election, it followeth unavoidably; for whether you take it as relating to this, of distinguishing between persons as touching the world to come, or with reference to God's acts of choosing this or that man to this or that office, work, or employment in this world, it still signifieth such a choosing, as that but some are therein concerned, and that therefore *some* are thence excluded. Are all the elect, the seed, the saved, the vessels of mercy, the chosen and peculiar? Are not some, yea the most, the children of the flesh, the rest, the lost, the vessels of wrath, of dishonour, and the children of perdition? Ro. xi. 9. 1 Pe. ii. 8, 9. Mat. x. 16. 2 Sa. vi. 21. Ps. lxxviii. 67, 68. Jn. xv. 16. 2 Co. iv. 3. Ro. ix. 21, 22. Jn. xvii. 12.

CHAP. II.

What Reprobation is.

Having thus shewed you that there is such a thing as a reprobation, I come now to shew you what it is.   Which that I may do to your edification, I shall *First* shew you what this word reprobation signifieth in the general, as it concerneth persons temporary and visibly reprobate: *Second*, more particularly, as it concerneth persons that are eternally and invisibly reprobate.

First, Generally, As it concerneth persons temporarily and visibly reprobate, thus: To be reprobate is to be disapproved, void of judgment, and rejected, &c.   To be disapproved, that is, when the word condemns them, either as touching the faith or the holiness of the gospel; the which they must needs be, that are void of spiritual and heavenly judgment in the mysteries of the kingdom; a manifest token [that] they are rejected.   And hence it is that they are said to be reprobate or void of judgment concerning the faith; reprobate or void of judgment touching every good work; having a reprobate mind, to do those things that are not convenient, either as to faith or manners.

And hence it is again, that they are also said to be rejected of God, cast away, and the like. 2 Co. xiii. 6, 7. 2 Ti. iii. 8. Tit. i. 16. Ro. i. 28. Je. vi. 30. 1 Co. ix. 27.

I call this temporary visible reprobation, because these appear, and are detected by the word as such that are found under the above-named errors, and so adjudged without the grace of God. Yet it is possible for some of these, however for the present disapproved, through the blessed acts and dispensations of grace, not only to become visible saints, but also saved for ever. Who doubts but that he who now by examining himself, concerning faith, doth find himself, though under profession, graceless, may after that, he seeing his woeful state, not only cry to God for mercy, but find grace, and obtain mercy to help in time of need? though it is true, that for the most part the contrary is fulfilled on them.

Second, But to pass this, and more particularly to touch the eternal invisible reprobation, which I shall thus hold forth: It is to be passed by in, or left out of, God's election; yet so, as considered upright. In which position you have these four things considerable: 1. The act of God's election. 2. The negative of that act. 3. The persons reached by that negative. And, 4. Their qualification when thus reached by it.

1. For the first. This act of God in electing, it is a choosing or fore-appointing of some infallibly unto eternal life, which he also hath determined shall be brought to pass by the means that should be made manifest and efficacious to that very end. Ep. i. 3—5. 1 Pe. i. 2.

2. Now the negative of this act is, a passing by,

or a leaving of those not concerned in this act; a leaving of them, I say, without the bounds, and so the saving privileges of this act; as it followeth by natural consequence, that because a man chooseth but some, therefore he chooseth not all, but leaveth, as the negative of that act, all others whatsoever. Wherefore, as I said before, those not contained within this blessed act, are called the *rest* besides the election. 'The election hath obtained it, and the rest were blinded.'

3. The persons then that are contained under the negative of this act, they are those, and those only, that pass through this wicked world without the saving grace of God's elect; those, I say, that miss the most holy faith, which they in time are blest withal, who are fore-appointed unto glory.

4. And now for the qualification they were considered under, when this act of reprobation laid hold upon them, to wit, They were considered upright.

This is evident, From this consideration, that reprobation is God's act, even the negative of his choosing or electing, and none of the acts of God make any man a sinner. It is further evident by the similitude that is taken from the carriage of the potter in his making of his pots; for by this comparison the God of heaven is pleased to shew unto us the nature of his determining in the act of reprobation. 'Hath not the potter power over the clay, of the same lump?' &c. Ro. ix. 21. Consider a little, and you shall see that these three things do necessarily fall in, to complete the potter's action in every pot he makes.

(1.) A determination in his own mind what pot

to make of this or that piece of clay; a determination, I say, precedent to the fashion of the pot; the which is true in the highest degree, in him that is excellent in working; he determines the end, before the beginning is perfected: Is. xli. 22. xlvi. 10. 'For this *cause* (very purpose) have I raised thee up.' Ex. ix. 16.

(2.) The next thing considerable in the potter; it is the so making of the pot, even as he determined; a vessel to honour, or a vessel to dishonour. There is no confusion nor disappointment under the hand of this eternal God, his work is perfect, and every way doth answer to what he hath determined. De. xxxii 4.

(3.) Observe again, That whether the vessel be to honour or to dishonour, yet the potter makes it good, sound, and fit for service; his fore-determining to make this a vessel to dishonour, hath no persuasion at all with him to break or mar the pot: Which very thing doth well resemble the state of man as under the act of eternal reprobation, for 'God made man upright.' Ec. vii. 29.

From these conclusions then,

Consider, 1. That the simple act of reprobation, it is a leaving or passing by, not a cursing of the creature.

Consider, 2. Neither doth this act alienate the heart of God from the reprobate, nor tie him up from loving, favouring, or blessing of him; no, not from blessing of him with the gift of Christ, of faith, of hope, and many other benefits. It only denieth them that benefit, that will infallibly bring them to eternal life, and that in despite of all opposition; it only denieth so to bless them as the

elect themselves are blessed.   Abraham loved all
the children he had by all his wives, and gave them
portions also; but his choice blessing, as the fruit
of his chiefest love, he reserved for chosen Isaac.
Ge. xxv. 5, 6.

Consider Lastly, The act of reprobation doth
harm to no man, neither means him any; nay, it
rather decrees him upright, lets him be made upright, and so be turned into the world.*

---

* As election took place before the creation of man—all
men in Adam were decreed, made and turned into the world
upright.—ED.

CHAP. III.

Of the Antiquity of Reprobation.

Having now proceeded so far as to shew you what reprobation is, it will not be amiss if in this place I briefly shew you its antiquity, even when it began its rise; the which you may gather by these following particulars.

First, Reprobation is before the person cometh into the world, or hath done good or evil: This is evident by that of Paul to the Romans: 'For *the children* being not yet born, neither having done any good or evil, that the purpose of God according to election might stand not of works, but of him that calleth; it was said unto Rebecca, The elder shall serve the younger.' ix. 11. Here you find twain in their mother's womb, and both receiving their destiny, not only before they had done good or evil, but before they were in a capacity to do it, they being yet unborn; their destiny, I say, the one unto, the other not unto, the blessing of eternal life; the one chose, the other refused; the one elect, the other reprobate. The same also might be said of Ishmael and his brother Isaac, both which did also receive their destiny before they came into the world: for the promise that this Isaac should be the heir, it was also before Ishmael was born, though he was elder by fourteen years, or more, than his brother. Ge. xv. 4, 5; xvi. 4, 5, 16; xvii. 25; xxi. 5. And it is yet further evident,

1. Because election is an act of grace; 'There is a remnant according to the election of grace.' Ro. xi. 5. Which act of grace saw no way so fit to discover its purity and independency, as by fastening on the object before it came into the world; that being the state in which at least no good were done, either to procure good from God, or to eclipse and darken this precious act of grace. For though it is true that no good thing that we have done before conversion, can obtain the grace of election; yet the grace of election then appeareth most, when it prevents† our doing good, that we might be loved therefore: wherefore he saith again, 'That the purpose of God according to election might stand, not of works, but of him that calleth; it was said unto her, The elder shall serve the younger.' Ro. ix. 11, 12.

2. This is most agreeable to the nature of the promise of giving seed to Abraham; which promise, as it was made before the child was conceived, so it was fulfilled at the best time, for the discovery of the act of grace, that could have been pitched

---

† 'Prevents our doing good.' Few words in the English language have more altered in their meaning than 'prevent;' it is derived from 'prævenio,' to go before. In Bunyan's time, it meant 'to go before,' 'clear the way,' 'make the way easy' for our doing good. Its present meaning is 'to obstruct,' by going or standing before us.—Ed.

upon: At this time will I come (saith God) 'and Sarah shall have a son;' Ge. xviii. 14. which promise, because it carried in its bowels the very grace of electing love, therefore it left out Ishmael, with the children of Keturah: 'For in Isaac shall thy seed be called.' Ro. iv. 16—19; ix. 7.

3. This was the best and fittest way for the decrees to receive sound bottom, even for God both to choose and refuse, before the creature had done good or evil, and so before they came into the world: 'That the purpose of God according to election might stand,' saith he, therefore before *the children* were yet born, or had done any good or evil, it was said unto her, &c. God's decree would for ever want foundation, should it depend at all upon the goodness and holiness either of men or angels; especially if it were to stand upon that good that is wrought before conversion, yea, or after conversion either. We find, by daily experience, how hard and difficult it is, for even the holiest in the world, to bear up and maintain their faith and love to God; yea, so hard, as not at all to do it without continual supplies from heaven. How then is it possible for any so to carry it before God, as to lay, by this his holiness, a foundation for election, as to maintain that foundation, and thereby to procure all those graces that infallibly saveth the sinner? But now the choice, I say, being a choice of grace, as is manifest, it being acted before the creature's birth; here grace hath laid the corner-stone, and determined the means to bring the work to perfection. Thus 'the foundation of God standeth sure, having this seal, The Lord knoweth them that are his:' 2 Ti. ii. 19. That

is, who he hath chosen, having excluded works, both good and bad, and founded all in an unchangeable act of grace; the negative whereof, is this harmless reprobation.

Second, But secondly, To step a little backward, and so to make all sure: This act of reprobation was before the world began; which therefore must needs confirm that which was said but now, that they were, before they were born, both destinated before they had done good or evil. This is manifest by that of Paul to the Ephesians, at the beginning of his epistle; where, speaking of Election, whose negative is reprobation, he saith, 'God hath chosen us in Christ before the foundation of the world.' Nay further, if you please, consider, that as Christ was ordained to suffer before the foundation of the world, and as we that are elected were chosen in him before the foundation of the world; so it was also ordained we should know him, before the foundation of the world; ordained that we should be holy before him in love, before the foundation of the world; and that we in time should be created in him to good works, and ordained before that we should walk in them. Wherefore reprobation also, it being the negative of electing love; that is, because God elected but some, therefore he left the rest: these rest therefore must needs be of as ancient standing under reprobation, as the chosen are under election; both which, it is also evident, was before the world began. Which serveth yet further to prove that reprobation could not be with respect to this or the other sin, it being only a leaving them, and that before the world, out of that free choice which he was pleased to bless the other with.   Even as the clay with which the dishonourable vessel is made, did not provoke the potter, for the sake of this or that impediment, *therefore* to make it so; but the potter of his own will, of the clay of the same lump, of the clay that is full as good as that of which he hath made the vessel to honour, did make this and the other a vessel of dishonour, &c. 1 Pe. i. 20, 21. 1 Co. ii. 7. Ep. i. 3, 4; ii. 10.*

---

* They who diligently attend to the scriptures, will find throughout the whole a vein of election and reprobation. The holy seed may be traced in many instances, and in divers families, in the Bible, from Adam to the birth of our Saviour, whose ancestors, according to the flesh, were of the line of election or the godly; which those who are only born after the flesh, and not after the Spirit, namely, the reprobate, have always despised and persecuted, and will do so to the end of time.—*Mason and Ryland.*

CHAP. IV.

Of the causes of Reprobation.

Having thus in a word or two shewed .the antiquity of Reprobation, I now come in this place to shew you the cause thereof; for doubtless this must stand a truth, That whatever God doth, there is sufficient ground therefore, whether by us apprehended, or else without our reach.

First then, It is caused from the very nature of God. There are two things in God, from which, or by the virtue of which, all things have their rise, to wit, the eternity of God in general, and the eternal perfection of every one of his attributes in particular: for as by the first, he must needs be before all things; so by virtue of the second, must all things consist. And as he is before all things, they having consistence by him; so also is he before all states, or their causes, be they either good or bad, of continuance or otherwise, he being the first without beginning, &c., whereas all other things, with their causes, have rise, dependance, or toleration of being from him. Col. i. 17.

Hence it follows, that nothing, either person or

cause, &c., can by any means have a being, but first he knows thereof, allows thereof, and decrees it shall be so. 'Who *is* he *that* saith, and it cometh to pass, *when* the Lord commandeth *it* not?' La. iii. 37. Now then, because that reprobation, as well as election, are subordinate to God; his will also, which is eternally perfect, being most immediately herein concerned; it was impossible that any should be reprobate, before God had both willed and decreed it should be so. It is not the being of a thing that administers matter of knowledge or foresight thereof to God, but the perfection of his knowledge, wisdom, and power, &c., that giveth the thing its being: God did not fore-decree there should be a world, because he foresaw there would be one; but there must be one, because he had before decreed there should be one. The same is true as touching the case in hand: 'For this cause [very purpose] have I raised thee up, for to shew *in* thee my power.' Ex. ix. 16. Ro. ix. 17.

Second, A second cause of eternal reprobation, is the exercise of God's sovereignty; for if this is true, that there is nothing either visible or invisible, whether in heaven or earth, but hath its being from him: then it must most reasonably follow, that he is therefore sovereign Lord, &c., and may also according to his own will, as he pleaseth himself, both exercise and manifest the same; being every whit absolute; and can do and may do whatsoever his soul desireth: and indeed, good reason, for he hath not only made them all, but 'for his pleasure they both were and are created.' Re. iv. 11.

Now the very exercise of this sovereignty produceth reprobation: 'Therefore hath he mercy on whom he will *have mercy*, and whom he will he hardeneth.' Ro. ix. 18. 'Hath not the potter power over the clay, of the same lump?' And doth he not make his pots according to his pleasure? Here therefore the mercy, justice, wisdom and power of God, take liberty to do what they will; saying, 'My counsel shall stand, and I will do all my pleasure.' Is. xlvi. 10. Job xxiii. 13. Da. iv. 35. Is. xliii. 13.

Third, Another cause of eternal reprobation, is the act and working of distinguishing love, and everlasting grace. God hath universal love, and particular love; general love, and distinguishing love; and so accordingly doth decree, purpose, and determine: from general love, the extension of general grace and mercy: but from that love that is distinguishing, peculiar grace and mercy: 'Was not Esau Jacob's brother?' saith the Lord, 'yet I loved Jacob.' Mal. i. 2. Yet I loved Jacob, that is, with a better love, or a love that is more distinguishing. As he further makes appear in his answer to our father Abraham, when he prayed to God for Ishmael: 'As for Ishmael, (saith he,) I have heard thee: Behold, I have blessed him, and will make him fruitful. But my covenant will I establish with Isaac, which Sarah shall bear unto thee.' Ge. xvii. 20, 21. Touching which words, there are these things observable.

1. That God had better love for Isaac, than he had for his brother Ishmael. Yet,

2. Not because Isaac had done more worthy and goodly deeds, for Isaac was yet unborn.

3. This choice blessing could not be denied to Ishmael, because he had disinherited himself by sin; for this blessing was entailed to Isaac, before

Ishmael had a being also. Ro. iv. 16—19. Ge. xv. 4, 5; xvi.

4. These things therefore must needs fall out through the working of distinguishing love and mercy, which had so cast the business, 'that the purpose of God according to election might stand.'

Further, Should not God decree to shew distinguishing love and mercy, as well as that which is general and common, he must not discover his best love at all to the sons of men. Again, if he should reveal and extend his best love to all the world in general, then there would not be such a thing as love that doth distinguish; for distinguishing love appeareth in separating between Isaac and Ishmael, Jacob and Esau, the many called, and the few chosen. Thus by virtue of distinguishing love, some must be reprobate: for distinguishing love must leave some, both of the angels in heaven, and the inhabitants of the earth; wherefore the decree also that doth establish it, must needs leave some.

Fourth, Another cause of reprobation, Is God's willingness to shew his wrath, and to make his power known. This is one of those arguments that the holy apostle setteth against the most knotty and strong objection that ever was framed against the doctrine of eternal reprobation: 'Thou wilt say then unto me, (saith he,) Why doth he yet find fault?' For if it be his will that some should be rejected, hardened, and perish, why then is he offended that any sin against him; 'for who hath resisted his will?' Hold, saith the apostle; stay a little here; first remember this, Is it meet to say unto God, What doest thou? 'Shall the thing formed say to him that formed *it*, Why hast thou made me thus?   Hath not the potter power over the clay, of the same lump,' &c.   Besides, when you have thought your worst, to wit, that the effects of reprobation must needs be consummate in the eternal perdition of the creature; yet again consider, ' *What* if God, willing to shew *his* wrath,' as well as grace and mercy?   And what if he, that he may so do, exclude some from having share in that grace that would infallibly, against all resistance, bring us safe unto eternal life? What then?   Is he therefore the author of your perishing, or his eternal reprobation either?   Do you not know that he may refuse to elect who he will, without abusing of them?   Also that he may deny to give them that grace that would preserve them from sin, without being guilty of their damnation? May he not, to shew his wrath, suffer ' with much long-suffering' all that are ' the vessels of wrath,' by their own voluntary will, to fit themselves for wrath and for destruction? Ro. ix. 19—22.   Yea, might he not even in the act of reprobation, conclude also to suffer them thus left, to fall from the state he left them in, that is, as they were considered upright; and when fallen, to bind them fast in chains of darkness unto the judgment of the great day, but he must needs be charged foolishly?   You shall see in that day what a harmony and what a glory there will be found in all God's judgments in the overthrow of the sinner; also how clear the Lord will shew himself of having any working hand in that which causeth eternal ruin; notwithstanding he hath reprobated such, doth suffer them to sin, and that too, that he might shew his wrath on the vessels of his wrath; the which I also, after this next chapter, shall further clear up to you. As 'the Lord knoweth how to deliver the godly out of temptations,' without approving of their miscarriages; so he also knoweth how 'to reserve the unjust unto the day of judgment to be punished:' 2 Pe. ii. 9. yet never to deserve the least of blame for his so reserving of them; though none herein can see his way, for he alone knows how to do it.*

---

* It is of God's mere mercy and grace that any sinners are called and admitted to the privilege of justification and adoption, upon God's own terms. The reason why the sinful and unworthy heathen (of whom Britain is a part) were called to be a people, who were not a people, while the Jews were left out and cast off for their obstinate unbelief, was not because the Gentiles were either more worthy or more willing (for they were all dead in trespasses and sins), but from God's discriminating grace and mercy.—*Mason and Ryland.*

CHAP. V.

Of the Unchangeableness of Eternal Reprobation.

Many opinions have passed through the hearts of the sons of men concerning reprobation; most of them endeavouring so to hold it forth, as therewith they might, if not heal their conscience slightly, yet maintain their own opinion, in their judgment, of other things; still wringing, now the word this way, and anon again that, for their purpose; also framing within their soul such an imagination of God and his acts in eternity, as would suit with such opinions, and so present all to the world. And the rather they have with greatest labour strained unweariedly at this above many other truths, because of the grim and dreadful face it carrieth in most men's apprehensions. But none of these things, however they may please the creature, can by any means in any measure, either cause God to undo, unsay, or undetermine what he hath concerning this, decreed and established.

First, Because they suit not with his nature, especially in these foundation-acts: 'The foundation of God standeth sure,' 2 Ti. ii. 19. even touching reprobation, 'that the purpose of God according to election might stand.' Ro. ix. 11. 'I know (saith Solomon) that whatsoever God doeth, it shall be for ever: nothing can be put to it, nor any thing taken from it,' &c. Ec. iii. 14. 'Hath he said, and shall he not do *it?* Hath he spoken, and shall he not make it good?' Nu. xxiii. 19. His decrees are composed according to his eternal wisdom, established upon his unchangeable will, governed by his knowledge, prudence, power, justice, and mercy, and are brought to conclusion, on his part, in perfect holiness, through the abiding of his most blessed truth and faithfulness: '*He is* the rock, his work *is* perfect: for all his ways are judgment: a God of truth and without iniquity, just and right *is* he.' De. xxxii. 4.

Second, This decree is made sure by the number, measure, and bounds of election; for election and reprobation do inclose all reasonable creatures; that is, either the one or the other; election, those that are set apart for glory; and reprobation, those left out of this choice.

Now as touching the elect, they are by this decree confined to that limited number of persons that must amount to the complete making up the fulness of the mystical body of Christ; yea so confined by this eternal purpose, that nothing can be diminished from or added thereunto: and hence it is that they are called his body and members in particular, 'the fulness of him that filleth all in all.' Ep. i. 23. and 'the measure of the stature of the fulness of Christ.' Ep. iv. 13. Which body, considering him as the head thereof, in conclusion maketh up one perfect man, and holy temple for the Lord.

These are called Christ's substance, inheritance and lot; Ps. xvi. and are said to be booked, marked, and sealed with God's most excellent knowledge, approbation and liking. 2 Ti. ii. 19.   As Christ said to his Father, 'Thine eyes did see my substance, yet being unperfect; and in thy book all *my members* were written, *which* in continuance were fashioned, when *as yet there was* none of them.' Ps. cxxxix. 16.   This being thus, I say, it is in the first place impossible that any of those members should miscarry, for 'Who shall lay any thing to the charge of God's elect?' Ro. viii. 33. and because they are as to number every way sufficient, being his body, and so by their completing to be made a perfect man: therefore all others are rejected, that the 'purpose of God according to election might stand.' Ro. ix. 11.   Besides, it would not only argue weakness in the decree, but monstrousness in the body, if after this, any appointed should miscarry, or any besides them be added to them. Mat. xxiv. 24.

Third, Nay further, that all may see how punctual, exact, and to a tittle this decree of election is, God hath not only as to number and quantity confined the persons, but also determined and measured, and that before the world, the number of the gifts and graces that are to be bestowed on these members in general; and also what graces and gifts to be bestowed on this or that member in particular: He 'hath blessed us with all spiritual blessings - in Christ, according as he hath chosen us in him before the foundation of the word;' Ep. i. 3, 4. And bestoweth them in time upon us, 'According to the eternal purpose which he

purposed in Christ Jesus our Lord:' Ep. iii. 11. He
hath given to the eye, the grace that belongeth to
the eye; and to the hand that which he also hath
appointed for it. And so to every other member
of the body elect, he doth deal out to them their
determined measure of grace and gifts most fit for
their place and office. Thus is the decree established, both of the saved, and also the non-elect.
Ro. xii. 3. Ep. iv. 16. Col. ii. 19. Ep. iv. 12, 13.

Fourth, But again, another thing that doth establish this decree of eternal reprobation, is the
weakness that sin, in the fall, and since, hath
brought all reprobates into: For though it be most
true, that sin is no cause of eternal reprobation;
yet seeing sin hath seized on the reprobate, it cannot be but thereby the decree must needs be the
faster fixed. If the king, for this or the other
weighty reason, doth decree not to give this or that
man, who yet did never offend him, a place in his
privy chamber; if this man after this shall be infected with the plague, this rather fastens than
loosens the king's decree. As the angels that
were left out of God's election, by reason of the
sin they committed after, are so far off from being
by that received into God's decree, that they are
therefore bound for it in chains of everlasting
darkness to the judgment of the great day.

Whether to be reprobated be the same with being appointed before-hand unto eternal condemnation? If not, how do they differ? Also whether reprobation be the cause of condemnation?

It hath been the custom of ignorant men much to quarrel at eternal reprobation, concluding, for want of knowledge in the mystery of God's will, that if he reprobate any from eternity, he had as good have said, I will make this man to damn him; I will decree this man, without any consideration, to the everlasting pains of hell. When in very deed, for God to reprobate, and to appoint before-hand to eternal condemnation, are two distinct things, properly relating to two distinct attributes, arising from two distinct causes.

First, They are two distinct things: Reprobation, a simple leaving of the creature out of the bounds of God's election; but to appoint to condemnation is to bind them over to everlasting punishment. Now there is a great difference between my refusing to make of such a tree a pillar in my house, and of condemning it unto the fire to be burned.

Second, As to the attributes; reprobation respects God's sovereignty; but to appoint to condemnation, his justice. Ro. ix. 18. Ge. xviii. 25.

Third, As to the causes; sovereignty being according to the will of God, but justice according to the sin of man. For God, though he be the only sovereign Lord, and that to the height of perfection; yet he appointeth no man to the pains of everlasting fire, merely from sovereignty, but by the rule of justice: God damneth not the man because he is a man, but a sinner; and fore-appoints him to that place and state, by fore-seeing of him wicked. Ro. i. 18, 19. Col. iii. 6.

Again, As reprobation is not the same with fore-appointing to eternal condemnation; so neither is it the cause thereof.

If it be the cause, then it must either, 1. Leave him infirm. Or, 2. Infuse sin into him. Or, 3. Take from him something that otherwise would keep him upright. 4. Or both license Satan to tempt, and the reprobate to close in with the temptation. But it doth none of these; therefore it is not the cause of the condemnation of the creature.

That it is not the cause of sin, it is evident,

1. Because the elect are as much involved therein, as those that are passed by.

2. It leaveth him not infirm; for he is by an after-act, to wit, of creation, formed perfectly upright.

3. That reprobation infuseth no sin, appeareth, because it is the act of God.

4. That it taketh nothing, that good is, from him, is also manifest, it being only a leaving of him.

5. And that it is not by this act that Satan is permitted to tempt, or the reprobate to sin, is manifest; because as Christ was tempted, so the elect fall as much into the temptation, at least many of them, as many of those that are reprobate: whereas if these things came by reprobation, then the reprobate would be only concerned therein. All which will be further handled in these questions yet behind.

Object. From what hath been said, there is concluded this at least, That God hath infallibly determined, and that before the world, the infallible damnation of some of his creatures: for if God hath before the world [was made] bound some over to eternal punishment, and that as you say, for sin; then this determination must either be fallible or infallible; not fallible, for then your other position of the certainty of the number of God's elect, is shaken; unless you hold that there may be a number that shall neither go to heaven nor hell. Well then, if God hath indeed determined, fore-determined, that some must infallibly perish; doth not this his determination lay a necessity on the reprobate to sin, that he may be damned; for, no sin, no damnation; that is your own argument.

Ans. That God hath ordained, (Jude 4.) the damnation of some of his creatures, it is evident; but whether this his determination be positive and absolute, there is the question: for the better understanding whereof, I shall open unto you the variety of God's determinations, and their nature, as also rise.

The determinations of God touching the destruction of the creature, they are either ordinary or extraordinary: those I count ordinary that were commonly pronounced by the prophets and apostles, &c., in their ordinary way of preaching; to the end men might be affected with the love of their own salvation: now these either bound or loosed, but as the condition or qualification was answered by the creature under sentence, and no otherwise. 1 Sa. xii. 25. Is. i. 20. Mat. xviii. 3. Lu. xiii. 1, 2, 3. Ro. ii. 8, 9; viii. 13; xi. 23. 1 Co. vi. 9—11.

Again, These extraordinary, though they respect the same conditions, yet they are not grounded immediately upon them, but upon the infallible fore-knowledge and fore-sight of God, and are thus distinguished. First the ordinary determination, it stands but at best upon a supposition that the creature may continue in sin, and admits of a possibility that it may not; but the extraordinary stands upon an infallible fore-sight that the creature will continue in sin; wherefore this must needs be positive, and as infallible as God himself.

Again, These two determinations are also distinguished thus: the ordinary is applicable to the elect as well as to the reprobate, but the other to the reprobate only. It is proper to say even to the elect themselves, 'He that believeth shall be saved, and he that believeth not shall be damned;' but not to say to them, These are appointed to UTTER destruction, or that they shall utterly perish in their own corruptions; or that for them is reserved the blackness of darkness for ever. 1 Ki. xx. 42. 2 Pe. ii. 12. Jude 13.

So then, though God by these determinations doth not lay some under irrecoverable condemnation, yet by one of them he doth; as is further made out thus:

1. God most perfectly foreseeth the final impenitency of those that so die, from the beginning to the end of the world. Pr. xv. 11. Ps. cxxxix. 2. Is. xlvi. 10.

2. Now from this infallible foresight, it is most easy and rational to conclude, and that positively, the infallible overthrow of every such creature. Did I infallibly foresee that this or that man would cut out his heart in the morning, I might infallibly determine his death before night.

Object. But still the question is, Whether God by this his determination doth not lay a necessity on the creature to sin? For, no sin, no condemnation: this is true by your own assertion.

Ans. No, by no means: for,

1. Though it be true, that sin must of absolute necessity go before the infallible condemnation and overthrow of the sinner; and that it must also be pre-considered by God; yet it needs not lay a necessity upon him to sin: for let him but alone to do what he will, and the determination cannot be more infallible than the sin, which is the cause of its execution.

2. As it needs not, so it doth not: for this positive determination is not grounded upon what God will effect, but on what the creature will; and that not through the instigation of God, but the instigation of the devil. What? might not I, if I most undoubtedly foresaw that such a tree in my garden would only cumber the ground, notwithstanding reasonable means, might not I, I say, from hence determine, seven years before, to cut it down, and burn it in the fire, but I must, by so determining, necessitate this tree to be fruitless? the case in hand is the very same. God therefore may most positively determine the infallible damnation of his creature, and yet not at all necessitate the creature to sin, that he might be damned.

Object. But how is this similitude pertinent? For God did not only foresee sin would be the destruction of the creature, but let it come into the world, and so destroy the creature. If you, as you foresee the fruitlessness of your tree, should withal see that which makes it so, and that too before it makes it so, and yet let the impediment come and make it so; are not you now the cause of the unfruitfulness of that tree which you have before condemned to the fire to be burned? for

God might have chose whether he would have let Adam sin, and so sin to have got into the world by him.

Ans. Similitudes never answer every way; if they be pertinent to that for which they are intended, it is enough; and to that it answereth well, being brought to prove no more but the natural consequence of a true and infallible foresight. And now as to what is objected further, as that God might have chose whether sin should have come into the world by Adam, to the destruction of so many: to that I shall answer,

1. That sin could not have come into the world without God's permission, it is evident, both from the perfection of his foresight and power.

2. Therefore all the means, motives, and inducements thereunto, must also by him be not only foreseen, but permitted.

3. Yet so, that God will have the timing, proceeding, bounding, and ordering thereof, at his disposal: 'Surely the wrath of man shall praise thee, and the remainder of wrath shalt thou restrain.' Ps. lxxvi. 10. 1 Ki. xxii. 20—22. Jn. viii. 20. Lu. xxii. 51, 52.

4. Therefore it must needs come into the world, not without, but by the knowledge of God; not in despite of him, but by his suffering of it.

Object. But how then is he clear from having a hand in the death of him that perisheth?

Ans. Nothing is more sure than that God could have kept sin out of the world, if it had been his will; and this is also as true, that it never came into the world with his liking and compliance; and for this, you must consider that sin came into the world by two steps:

1. By being offered. 2. By prevailing.

Touching the first of these, God without the least injury to any creature in heaven or earth, might not only suffer it, but so far countenance the same: that is, so far forth as for trial only: as it is said of Abraham; 'God tempted Abraham' to slay his only son, Ge. xxii. 1. and led Christ by the Spirit into the wilderness to be tempted of the devil. Mar. i. 12. Lu. iv. 1. This is done without any harm at all; nay, it rather produceth good; for it tends to discover sincerity, to exercise faith in, and love to his Creator; also to put him in mind of the continual need he hath of depending on his God for the continuation of help and strength, and to provoke to prayers to God, whenever so engaged. De. viii. 1—3. 1 Pe. i. 7. He. v. 7. Mat. xxvi. 22, 41.

Object. But God did not only admit that sin should be offered for trial, and there to stay; but did suffer it to prevail, and overcome the world.

Ans. Well, this is granted: but yet consider,

1. God did neither suffer it, nor yet consent it should, but under this consideration; If Adam, upright Adam, gave way thereto, by forsaking his command, 'In the day that thou eatest thereof thou shalt surely die.' Ge. ii. 17; iii. 3. Which Adam did, not because God did compel him or persuade him to it, but voluntarily of his own mind, contrary to his God's command: so then, God by suffering sin to break into the world, did it rather in judgment, as disliking Adam's act, and as a punishment to man for listening to the tempter; and as a discovery of his anger at man's disobedience; than to prove that he is guilty of the misery of his creature.

2. Consider also, that when God permitted sin for trial, it was, when offered first, to them only

who were upright, and had sufficient strength to resist it.

3. They were by God's command to the contrary, driven to no strait to tempt them to incline to Satan: 'Of every tree of the garden thou mayest freely eat,' saith God; only let this alone.

4. As touching the beauty and goodness that was in the object unto which they were allured; What was it? Was it better than God? Yea, was it better than the tree of life? For from that they were not exempted till after they had sinned. Did not God know best what was best to do them good?

5. Touching him that persuaded them to do this wicked act; was his word more to be valued for truth, more to be ventured on for safety, or more to be honoured for the worthiness of him that spake, than was his that had forbad it? The one being the devil, with a lie, and to kill them; the other being God, with his truth, and to preserve them safe.

Quest. But was not Adam unexpectedly surprised? Had he notice beforehand, and warning of the danger? For God foresaw the business.

Ans. Doubtless God was fair and faithful to his creature in this thing also; as clearly doth appear from these considerations.

1. The very commandment that God gave him, fore-bespake him well to look about him; and did indeed insinuate that he was likely to be tempted.

2. It is yet more evident, because God doth even tell him of the danger; 'In the day that thou eatest thereof thou shalt surely die.'

3. Nay God by speaking to him of the very tree that was to be forborn, telling him also where it stood, that he might the better know it; did in

effect expressly say unto him, Adam, if thou be
tempted, it will be about that tree, and the fruit
thereof: wherefore if thou findest the tempter
there, then beware thy life.

(1.) To conclude then: though sin did not come
into the world without God's sufferance, yet it did
without his liking: God suffered also Cain to kill
his brother, and Ishmael to mock at Isaac, but he
did not like the same. Ge. iv. 9—11. Ga. iv. 30.

(2.) Therefore though God was first in concluding sin should be offered to the world; yet man
was the first that consented to a being overcome
thereby.

(3.) Then, Though God did fore-determine that
sin should enter, yet it was not but with respect
to certain terms and conditions, which yet was not
to be enforced by virtue of the determination, but
permitted to be completed by the voluntary inclination of a perfect and upright man. And in that
the determination was most perfectly infallible, it
was through the foresight of the undoubted inclination of this good and upright person.

Quest. But might not God have kept Adam from
inclining, if he would?

Ans. What more certain? But yet consider,

1. Adam being now an upright man, he was
able to have kept himself, had he but looked to it
as he should and might.

2. This being so, if God had here stept in, he
had either added that which had been needless,
and so had not obtained thankfulness; or else had
made the strength of Adam useless, yea his own
workmanship in so creating him, superfluous; or
else by consequence imperfect.

(3.) If he had done so, he had taken Adam from

his duty, which was to trust and believe his Maker; he had also made void the end of the commandment, which was to persuade to watchfulness, diligence, sobriety, and contentedness; yea, and by so doing would not only himself have tempted Adam to transgression, even to lay aside the exercise of that strength that God had already given him; but should have become the pattern, or the first father to all looseness, idleness, and neglect of duty. Which would also not only have been an ill example to Adam to continue to neglect so reasonable and wholesome duties, but would have been to himself an argument of defence to retort upon his God, when he had come at another time to reckon with him for his misdemeanours.*

Many other weighty reasons might here be further added for God's vindication in this particular, but at this time let these suffice.

* The final condemnation of the wicked does not spring from God's sovereign will to destroy any of his rational creatures; this is evident from the many pressing invitations, declarations, and promises in the word of God: for Jehovah swears by his great self, that he desires not the death of a sinner. Our Lord assigns the cause of reprobation in these words, John v. 40, 'Ye will not come unto me, that ye might have life;' wherefore Christ, the only remedy for their cure, being rejected, the sinner is condemned, and rendered the object of wrath and punishment by the law and justice of God; because the same word of truth which says, 'Whosoever will, let him come, and take of the water of life freely,' also says, 'The soul that sinneth (or lives and dies in sin unpardoned) shall die.' Thus sin is the object of God's hatred, and not the man, abstractedly considered. May we therefore each of us have grace to look to Christ for full and complete salvation, who hath put away sin by the sacrifice of himself, whereby he has perfected for ever them that are sanctified!—*Ryland and Mason*.

CHAP. VII.

Whether any under Eternal Reprobation have just cause to quarrel with God for not electing of them?

That the answer to this question may be to edification, recall again what I have before asserted; to wit, That for a man to be left out of God's election, and to be made a sinner, is two things; and again, For a man to be not elect, and to be condemned to hell-fire, is two things also. Now I say, if non-election makes no man a sinner, and if it appoints no man to condemnation neither, then what ground hath any reprobate to quarrel with God for not electing of him? Nay, further, reprobation considereth him upright, leaveth him upright, and so turneth him into the world; what wrong doth God do him, though he hath not elected him? What reason hath he that is left in this case to quarrel against his Maker?

If thou say, because God hath not chosen them, as well as chosen others: I answer, 'Nay but, O man, who art thou that repliest against God? Shall the thing formed say to him that formed *it*, Why hast thou made me thus?' Ro. ix. 20. 'Behold, as the clay *is* in the potter's hand, so *are* ye in my hand, O house of Israel,' saith the Lord God. Je. xviii. 6. So then, if I should say no more but that God is the only Lord and Creator, and that by his sovereignty he hath power to dispose of them according to his pleasure, either to choose or to refuse, according to the counsel of his own will, who could object against him and be guiltless? 'He giveth not account of any of his matters.' Job xxxiii. 13. 'And *what* his soul desireth, even *that* he doeth.' Job xxiii. 13.

Again, God is wiser than man, and therefore can shew a reason for what he acts and does, both when and where at present thou seest none. Shall God the only wise, be arraigned at the bar of thy blind reason, and there be judged and condemned for his acts done in eternity? Who hath directed the Spirit of the Lord, 'or who hath been his counsellor?' Ro. xi. 34. Do you not know that he is far more above us, than we are above our horse or mule that is without understanding? 'Great things doeth he, which we cannot comprehend.' Jo. xxxvii. 5. 'Great things and unsearchable, marvellous things without number.' Job v. 9.

But, I say, should we take it well if our beast should call us to account for this and the other righteous act, and judge us unrighteous, and our acts ridiculous, and all because it sees no reason for our so doing? Why, we are as beasts before God. Ps. lxxiii 22.

But again, to come yet more close to the point: the reprobate quarrels with God, because he hath not elected him; well, but is not God the master of his own love? And is not his will the only rule of his mercy? And may he not, without he give offence to thee, lay hold by electing love and mercy on whom himself pleaseth? Must thy reason, nay, thy lust, be the ruler, orderer, and disposer of his grace? 'Is it not lawful for me to do what I will with mine own?' saith he, 'Is thine eye evil, because I am good?' Mat. xx. 15.

Further, What harm doth God to any reprobate, by not electing of him; he was, as hath been said, considered upright, so formed in the act of creation, and so turned into the world: indeed he was not elected, but hath that taken anything from him? No, verily, but leaveth him in good condition: there is good, and better, and best of all; he that is in a good estate, though others through free grace are in a far better, hath not any cause to murmur either with him that gave him such a place, or at him that is placed above him. In a word, reprobation maketh no man personally a sinner, neither doth election make any man personally righteous. It is the consenting to sin that makes a man a sinner; and the imputation of grace and righteousness that makes [men] gospelly and personally just and holy.

But again, seeing it is God's act to leave some out of the bounds of his election, it must needs be, therefore, positively good: Is that then which is good in itself made sin unto thee? God forbid: God doth not evil by leaving this or that man out of his electing grace, though he choose others to eternal life, through Jesus Christ our Lord. Wherefore there is not a reprobate that hath any cause, and therefore no just cause, to quarrel with his

37

Maker, for not electing of him.

And that, besides what hath been spoken, if you consider,

1. For God to elect, is an act of sovereign grace; but to pass by, or to refuse so to do, is an act of sovereign power, not of injustice.

2. God might therefore have chosen whether he would have elected any, or so many or few; and also which and where he would.

3. Seeing then that all things are at his dispose, he may fasten electing mercy where he pleaseth; and other mercy, if he will, to whom and when he will.

4. Seeing also that the least of mercies are not deserved by the best of sinners; men, instead of quarrelling against the God of grace, because they have not what they list, should acknowledge they are unworthy of their breath; and also should confess that God may give mercy where he pleaseth, and that too, both which or what, as also to whom, and when he will; and yet be good, and just, and very gracious still: Nay, Job saith, 'He taketh away, who can hinder him? Who will say unto him, What doest thou?' Job ix. 12.

The will of God is the rule of all righteousness, neither knoweth he any other way by which he governeth and ordereth any of his actions. Whatsoever God doth, it is good because he doth it; whether it be to give grace, or to detain it; whether in choosing or refusing. The consideration of this, made the holy men of old ascribe righteousness to their Maker, even then when yet they could not see the reason of his actions. They would rather stand amazed, and wonder at the heights and depths of his unsearchable judgments, than quarrel at the strange and most obscure of them. Job xxxiv. 10—12; xxxvi. 3; xxxvii. 23. Je. xii. 1. Ro. xi. 33.

God did not intend that all that ever he would do, should be known to every man, no nor yet to the wise and prudent. It is as much a duty sometimes to stay ourselves and wonder, and to confess our ignorance in many things of God, as it is to do other things that are duty without dispute. So then, let poor dust and ashes forbear to condemn the Lord, because he goeth beyond them; and also they should beware they speak not wickedly for him, though it be, as they think, to justify his actions. ' The Lord *is* righteous in all his ways, and holy in all his works.'* Ps. cxlv. 17. Mat. xi. 25 1 Co. ii. 8. Job xiii. 6—8.

---

* 'Secret things belong to God, but those that are revealed belong to us.' It is a vain thing for men to cavil at the doctrine of peculiar election, and to quarrel with God for choosing some, and passing by others. Their best way would be to assure themselves of their own election, by using the means, and walking in the ways of God's appointment, as laid down in the word, and then they will find that God cannot deny himself, but will make good to them every promise therein; and thus, by scripture evidence, they will find that they are elected unto life, and will be thankful and humble. They will then find that an hearty affectionate trusting in Christ for all his salvation, as freely promised to us, hath naturally enough in it to work in our souls a natural bent and inclination to, and ability for, the practice of all holiness.—*Ryland and Mason.*

CHAP. VIII.

Whether Eternal reprobation in itself, or in its doctrine, be in very deed an hindrance to any man in seeking the salvation of his soul.

In my discourse upon this question, I must entreat the reader to mind well what is premised in the beginning of the former chapter, which is, That reprobation makes no man a sinner, appoints no man to condemnation, but leaveth him upright after all. So then, though God doth leave the most of men without the bounds of his election, his so doing is neither in itself, nor yet its doctrine, in very deed, an hindrance to any man in seeking the salvation of his soul.

First, It hindereth not in itself, as is clear by the ensuing considerations :—

1. That which hindereth him is the weakness that came upon him by reason of sin. Now God only made the man, but man's listening to Satan made him a sinner, which is the cause of all his weakness: this therefore is it that hindereth him, and that also disenableth him in seeking the salvation of his soul. 'Let no man say when he is tempted, I am tempted of God: for God cannot be

tempted with evil, neither tempteth he any man.'
Ja. i. 13. 'God made man upright; but they have
sought out many inventions.' Ec. vii. 29. Eze. xvi. 30. Ho.
xiii. 9; xiv. 1. Ge. iii. 8—11.

2. It hindereth not in itself, for it taketh not
anything from a man that would help him, might
it continue with him; it takes not away the least
part of his strength, wisdom, courage, innocency,
or will to good; all these were lost by the fall, in
that day when he died the death. Nay, reprobation under some consideration did rather establish
all these upon the reprobate; for as it decrees him
left, so left upright. Wherefore man's hindrance
cometh on him from other means, even by the fall,
and not by the simple act of eternal reprobation.
Ge. iii.

3. As reprobation hindereth not either of these
two ways, so neither is it from this simple act that
Satan is permitted either to tempt them, that they
might be tried, or that they might be overthrown.

(1.) It is not by this act that Satan is permitted
to tempt them that they might be tried; because
then the Son of God himself must be reached by
this reprobation; he being tempted by the devil as
much, if not more than any. Yea, and then must
every one of the elect be under eternal reprobation; for they also, and that after their conversion,
are greatly assaulted by him. 'Many are the
troubles of the righteous,' &c. Mat. iv. 1, 2. He. ii. 17;
iv. 15.

(2.) Neither is it from the act of reprobation
that sin hath entered the world, no more than
from election, because those under the power of
election did not only fall at first, but do still gene-

rally as foully, before conversion, as the reprobate himself. Whereas, if either the temptation, or the fall, were by virtue of reprobation, then the reprobates, and they only, should have been tempted, and have fallen. The temptation then, and the fall, doth come from other means, and so the hinderance of the reprobate, than from eternal reprobation. For the temptation, the fall and hinderance being universal, but the act of reprobation particular, the hinderance must needs come from such a cause as taketh hold on all men, which indeed is the fall; the cause of which was neither election nor reprobation, but man's voluntary listening to the tempter. Ro. iii. 9.

(3.) It is yet far more evident that reprobation hindereth no man from seeking the salvation of his soul: because notwithstanding all that reprobation doth, yet God giveth to divers of the reprobates great encouragements thereto ; to wit, the tenders of the gospel in general, not excluding any; great light also to understand it, with many a sweet taste of the good word of God, and the powers of the world to come; he maketh them sometimes also to be partakers of the Holy Ghost, and admitteth many of them into fellowship with his elect ; yea, some of them to be rulers, teachers, and governors in his house: all which, without doubt, both are and ought to be great encouragements even to the reprobates themselves, to seek the salvation of their souls. Mat. xi. 28. Re. xxii. 17. He. vi. 4, 5. Mat. xxv. 1, 2. Ac. i. 16, 17.

Second, As it hindereth not in itself, so it hindereth not by its doctrine: for, all that this doctrine saith is, that some are left out of God's election, as considered upright. Now this doctrine cannot hinder any man.   For,

1. No man still stands upright.

2. Though it saith some are left, yet it points at no man, it nameth no man, it binds all faces in secret.   So then, if it hinder, it hindereth all, even the elect as well as reprobate; for the reprobate hath as much ground to judge himself elect, as the very elect himself hath, before he be converted, being both alike in a state of nature and unbelief, and both alike visibly liable to the curse, for the breach of the commandment.   Again, As they are equals here, so also have they ground alike to close in with Christ and live; even the open, free, and full invitation of the gospel, and promise of life and salvation, by the faith of Jesus Christ. Ep. ii. 1, 2. Ro. iii. 9. Jn. iii. 16. 2 Co. v. 19—21. Re. xxi. 6; xxii. 17.

3. It is evident also by experience, that this doctrine doth not, *in deed*, neither can it hinder any (this doctrine I mean, when both rightly stated and rightly used) because many who have been greatly afflicted about this matter, have yet at last had comfort; which comfort, when they have received it, hath been to them as an argument that the thing they feared before, was not because of reprobation rightly stated; but its doctrine much abused was the cause of their affliction: and had they had the same light at first they received afterwards, their troubles then would soon have fled, as also now they do.   Wherefore discouragement comes from want of light, because they are not skilful in the word of righteousness: for had the discouragement at first been true, which yet it could not be, unless the person knew

by name himself under eternal reprobation, which is indeed impossible, then his light would have pinched him harder; light would rather have fastened this his fear, than at all have rid him of it. He. v. 12—14.

Indeed the scripture saith, the word is to some the savour of death unto death, when to others the savour of life unto life. But mark, it is not this doctrine in particular, if so much as some other, that doth destroy the reprobate. It was respite at which Pharaoh hardened his heart; and the grace of God that the reprobates of old did turn into lasciviousness. Yea, Christ the Saviour of the world, is a stumbling-block unto some, and a rock of offence unto others. But yet again, consider that neither HE, nor any of God's doctrines, are so simply, and in their own true natural force and drift: for they beget no unbelief, they provoke to no wantonness, neither do they in the least encourage to impenitency; all this comes from that ignorance and wickedness that came by the fall: Wherefore it is by reason of that also, that they stumble, and fall, and grow weak, and are discouraged, and split themselves, either at the doctrine of reprobation, or at any other truth of God. Ex. viii. 15. Jude iv. 1. 1 Pe. ii. 8.

Lastly, To conclude as I began, there is no man while in this world, that doth certainly know, that he is left out of the electing love of the great God; neither hath he any word in the whole bible, to persuade him so to conclude and believe; for the scriptures hold forth salvation to the greatest of sinners. Wherefore, though the act of reprobation were far more harsh, and its doctrine also more sharp and severe, yet it cannot properly be said to hinder any. It is a foolish thing in any to be troubled with those things which they have no ground to believe concerns themselves; especially when the latitude of their discouragement is touching their own persons only. 'The secret *things belong* unto the Lord our God.' De. xxix. 29. Indeed every one of the words of God ought to put us upon examination, and into a serious enquiry of our present state and condition, and how we now do stand for eternity; to wit, whether we are ready to meet the Lord, or how it is with us. Yet, when search is fully made, and the worst come unto the worst, the party can find himself no more than the chief of sinners, not excluded from the grace of God tendered in the gospel; not from an invitation, nay a promise, to be embraced and blest, if he comes to Jesus Christ. Wherefore he hath no ground to be discouraged by the doctrine of reprobation. 1 Ti. i. 15. Ac. iii. 19. 2 Ch. xxxiii. Jn. vii. 37; vi. 37. Mar. ii. 17.

CHAP. IX.

Whether God would indeed and in truth, that the gospel, with the grace thereof, should be tendered to those that yet he hath bound up under Eternal Reprobation ?

To this question I shall answer,

First, In the language of our Lord, 'Go preach the gospel unto every creature;' Mar. xvi. 15. and again, 'Look unto me, and be ye saved; all ye ends of the earth.' Is. xlv. 22. 'And whosoever will, let him take the water of life freely.' Re. xxii. 17. And the reason is, because Christ died for all, 'tasted death for every man;' 2 Co. v. 15. He. ii. 9. is 'the Saviour of the world,' 1 Jn. iv. 14. and the propitiation for the sins of the whole world.

Second, I gather it from those several censures that even every one goeth under, that doth not receive Christ, when offered in the general tenders of the gospel; 'He that believeth not, - shall be damned;' Mar. xvi. 16. 'He that believeth not God hath made him a liar, because he believeth not the record that God gave of his Son;' 1 Jn. v. 10. and, Woe unto thee Capernaum, 'Woe unto thee Chorazin! woe unto thee Bethsaida!' Mat. xi. 21. with many other sayings, all which words, with many other of the same nature, carry in them a very great argument to this very purpose; for if those that perish in the days of the gospel, shall have, at least, their damnation heightened, because they have neglected and refused to receive the gospel, it must needs be that the gospel was with all faithfulness to be tendered unto them; the which it could not be, unless the death of Christ did extend itself unto them; Jn. iii. 16. He. ii. 3. for the offer of the gospel cannot, with God's allowance, be offered any further than the death of Jesus Christ doth go; because if that be taken away, there is indeed no gospel, nor grace to be extended. Besides, if by every creature, and the like, should be meant only the elect, then are all the persuasions of the gospel to no effect at all; for still the unconverted, who are here condemned for refusing of it, they return it as fast again: I do not know I am elect, and therefore dare not come to Jesus Christ; for if the death of Jesus Christ, and so the general tender of the gospel, concern the elect alone; I, not knowing myself to be one of that number, am at a mighty plunge; nor know I whether is the greater sin, to believe, or to despair: for I say again, if Christ died only for the elect, &c. then, I not knowing myself to be one of that number, dare not believe the gospel, that holds forth his blood to save me; nay, I think with safety may not, until I first do know I am elect of God, and appointed thereunto.

Third, God the Father, and Jesus Christ his Son, would have all men whatever, invited by the gospel to lay hold of life by Christ, whether elect or reprobate; for though it be true, that there is such a thing as election and reprobation, yet God, by the tenders of the gospel in the ministry of his word, looks upon men under another consideration, to wit, as sinners; and as sinners invites them to believe, lay hold of, and embrace the same. He saith not to his ministers, Go preach to the elect, because they are elect; and shut out others, because they are not so: But, Go preach the gospel to sinners as sinners; and as they are such, go bid them come to me and live. And it must needs be so, otherwise the preacher could neither speak in faith, nor the people hear in faith. First, the preacher could not speak in faith, because he knoweth not the elect from the reprobate; nor they again hear in faith, because, as unconverted, they would be always ignorant of that also. So then, the minister neither knowing whom he should offer life unto, nor yet the people which of them are to receive it; how could the word now be preached in faith with power? And how could the people believe and embrace it? But now the preacher offering mercy in the gospel to sinners, as they are sinners, here is way made for the word to be spoke in faith, because his hearers are sinners; yea, and encouragement also for the people to receive and close therewith, they understanding they are sinners: 'Christ Jesus came into the world to save sinners.' 1 Ti. i. 15. Lu. xxiv. 46, 47.

Fourth, The gospel must be preached to sinners as they are sinners, without distinction of elect or reprobate; because neither the one nor yet the other, as considered under these simple acts, are fit subjects to embrace the gospel: for neither the one act, nor yet the other, doth make either of them sinners; but the gospel is to be tendered to men as they are sinners, and personally under the curse of God for sin: wherefore to proffer grace to the elect because they are elect, it is to proffer grace and mercy to them, as not considering them as sinners. And, I say, to deny it to the reprobate, because he is not elected, it is not only a denial of grace to them that have no need thereof, but also before occasion is given on their part, for such a dispensation.   And I say again, therefore, to offer Christ and grace to man elect, as simply so considered, this administers to him no comfort at all, he being here no sinner; and so engageth not the heart at all to Jesus Christ; for that comes in, and is effected on them as they are sinners. Yea, to deny the gospel also to the reprobate, because he is not elect, it will not trouble him at all; for saith he, So I am not a sinner, and so do not need a Saviour.   But now, because the elect have no need of grace in Christ by the gospel, but as they are sinners; nor the reprobates cause to refuse it, but as they are sinners; therefore Christ by the word of the gospel, is to be proffered to both, without considering elect or reprobate, even as they are sinners.   'The whole have no need of the physician, but they that are sick: I came not to call the righteous, but sinners to repentance.' Mar. ii. 17. 2 Co. v. 14, 15. Lu. vii. 47.

Thus you see the gospel is to be tendered to all in general, as well to the reprobate as to the elect, TO SINNERS AS SINNERS; and so are they to receive it, and to close with the tenders thereof.*

* None are excluded the benefit of the great and precious salvation procured and finished by the Lord Jesus Christ, but they, who by perverseness, unbelief, and impenitency, exclude themselves.   Sinners,—miserable, helpless, and hopeless sinners, are the objects of this salvation: whosoever is enabled to see, in the light of God's Spirit, their wretched and forlorn state; to feel their want of Christ as a suitable Saviour, and to repent and forsake their sins, shall find mercy; for 'God is no respecter of persons,' Acts x. 34.—*Ryland and Mason.*

CHAP. X.

*Seeing then that the grace of God in the gospel, is
by that to be proffered to sinners, as sinners; as
well to the reprobate as the elect; Is it possible for
those who indeed are not elect, to receive it, and
be saved ?*

To this question I shall answer several things:
but *first* I shall shew you what that grace is, that
is tendered in the gospel; and *secondly*, what it is
to receive it and be saved.

First then, The grace that is offered to sinners
as sinners, without respect to this or that person,
it is a sufficiency of righteousness, pardoning grace,
and life, laid up in the person of Christ, held forth
in the exhortation and word of the gospel, and
promised to be theirs that receive it; yea, I say,
in so universal a tender, that not one is by it excluded or checked in the least, but rather encou-
raged, if he hath the least desire to life; yea, it is
held forth to beget both desires and longings after
the life thus laid up in Christ, and held forth by
the gospel. Jn. i. 16. Col. i. 19, 23. 1 Jn. v. 11, 12. Ac. xiii. 38, 39.
Ro. x. 12—14.; xvi. 25, 26.

Secondly, To receive this grace thus tendered by
the gospel, it is,

1. To believe it is true.

2. To receive it heartily and unfeignedly through faith.   And,

3. To let it have its natural sway, course and authority in the soul, and that in that measure, as to bring forth the fruits of good living in heart, word, and life, both before God and man.

Now then to the question.

Is it possible that this tender, thus offered to the reprobate, should by him be thus received and embraced, and he live thereby ?

To which I answer in the negative. Nor yet for the elect themselves, I mean as considered dead in trespasses and sins, which is the state of all men, elect as well as reprobate. So then, though there be a sufficiency of life and righteousness laid up in Christ for all men, and this tendered by the gospel to them without exception; yet sin coming in between the soul and the tender of this grace, it hath in truth disabled all men, and so, notwithstanding this tender, they continue to be dead. For the gospel, I say, coming in word only, saveth no man, because of man's impediment; wherefore those that indeed are saved by this gospel, the word comes not to them in word only, but also in power, and in the Holy Ghost; is mixed with faith, even with the faith of the operation of God, by whose exceeding great and mighty power they are raised from this death of sin, and enabled to embrace the gospel.   Doubtless, all men being dead in trespasses and sins, and so captivated under the power of the devil, the curse of the law, and shut up in unbelief; it must be the power of God, yea the exceeding greatness of that power that raiseth the soul from this condition, to receive the holy gospel. Ep. ii. 1—3. 1 Th. i. 5, 6. Col. ii. 12. He. iv. 1, 2. Ep. i. 18, 19. &c.

For man by nature, (consider him at best), can see no more, nor do no more than what the principles of nature understands and helps to do; which nature being below the discerning of things truly, spiritually, and savingly good, it must needs fall short of receiving, loving and delighting in them. 'The natural man receiveth not the things of the Spirit of God, for they are foolishness unto him: neither can he know *them*, because they are spiritually discerned.' 1 Co. ii. 14. Now I say, if the natural man at best (for the elect before conversion are no more, if quite so much) cannot do this, how shall they attain thereto, being now not only corrupted and infected, but depraved, bewitched and dead; swallowed up of unbelief, ignorance, confusion, hardness of heart, hatred of God, and the like? When a thorn by nature beareth grapes, and a thistle beareth figs, then may this thing be. Mat. vii. 16—18. To lay hold of and receive the gospel by a true and saving faith, it is an act of the soul as made a new creature, which is the workmanship of God: 'Now he that hath wrought us for the self-same thing *is* God.' 2 Co. v. 5. 'For a corrupt tree cannot bring forth good fruit.' Lu. vi. 43—45. 'Can the Ethiopian change his skin?' Je. xiii. 23.

But yet the cause of this impossibility.

1. Lieth not in reprobation, the elect themselves being as much unable to receive it as the other.

2. Neither is it because the reprobate is excluded in the tender, for that is universal.

3. Neither is it because there wanteth arguments

in the tenders of the gospel, for there is not only plenty, but such as be persuasive, clear, and full of rationality.

4. Neither is it because these creatures have no need thereof, for they have broken the law.

5. Wherefore it is, because indeed they are by sin dead, captivated, mad, self-opposers, blind, alienated in their minds, and haters of the Lord. Behold the ruins that sin hath made!

Wherefore whoever receiveth the grace that is tendered in the gospel, they must be quickened by the power of God, their eyes must be opened, their understandings illuminated, their ears unstopped, their hearts circumcised, their wills also rectified, and the Son of God revealed in them. Yet as I said, not because there wanteth argument in these tenders, but because men are dead, and blind, and cannot hear the word. 'Why do ye not understand my speech (saith Christ): *Even* because ye cannot hear my word.' Jn. viii. 43. Ac. ix. 15; xxvi. 9, 10. Ps. cx. 3. Ga. i. 15. Mat. xi. 27.

For otherwise, as I said but now, there is, 1. Rationality enough in the tenders of the gospel. 2. Persuasions of weight enough to provoke to faith. And, 3. Arguments enough to persuade to continue therein.

1. Is it not reasonable that man should believe God in the proffer of the gospel and life by it? Is there not reason, I say, both from the truth and faithfulness of God, from the sufficiency of the merits of Christ, as also from the freeness and fullness of the promise? What unreasonable thing doth the gospel bid thee credit? Or what falsehood doth it command thee to receive for truth?

Indeed in many points the gospel is above reason, but yet in never a one against it; especially in those things wherein it beginneth with the sinner, in order to eternal life.

2. Again, touching its persuasions to provoke to faith: With how many signs and wonders, miracles and mighty deeds, hath it been once and again confirmed, and that to this very end? He. i. 1—3. 1 Co. xiv. 22. With how many oaths, declarations, attestations, and proclamations, is it avouched, confirmed, and established? He. vi. 17, 18. Ac. xiii. 32. Je. iii. 12. Ga. iii. 15. And why should not credence be given to that gospel that is confirmed by blood, the blood of the Son of God himself? Yea, that gospel that did never yet fail any that in truth hath cast themselves upon it, since the foundation of the world. He. ix. 16—18. and xii. 1—3.

3. Again, as there is rationality enough, and persuasions sufficient, so there is also argument most prevalent to persuade to continue therein, and that to heartily, cheerfully, and unfeignedly, unto the end: did not, as I have said, blindness, madness, deadness, and wilful rebellion, carry them away in the vanity of their minds, and overcome them. Ep. iv. 17—19.

(1.) For, first, if they could but consider how they have sinned, how they have provoked God, &c., if they could but consider what a dismal state the state of the damned is, and also, that in a moment their condition is like to be the same, would they not cleave to the gospel and live?

(2.) The enjoyment of God, and Christ, and saints, and angels, being the sweetest; the pleasures of heaven the most comfortable, and to live always in the greatest height of light, life, joy, and gladness imaginable, one would think were enough to persuade the very damned now in hell.

There is no man then perisheth for want of sufficient reason in the tenders of the gospel, nor any for want of persuasions to faith; nor yet because there wanteth arguments to provoke to continue therein. But the truth is, the gospel in this hath to do with unreasonable creatures; with such as will not believe it, and that because it is truth: 'And because I tell *you* the truth, (saith Christ,) therefore ye believe me not.' Jn. viii. 45.

Quest. Well, but if this in truth be thus, how then comes it to pass that some receive it and live for ever? For you have said before, that the elect are as dead as the reprobate, and full as unable as they, as men, to close with these tenders, and live.

Answ. Doubtless this is true, and were the elect left to themselves, they, through the wickedness of their heart, would perish as do others. Neither could all the reasonable persuasive prevalent arguments of the gospel of God in Christ, prevail to make any receive it, and live. Wherefore here you must consider, that as there is mercy proclaimed in the general tenders of the gospel, so there is also the grace of election; which grace kindly overruleth and winneth the spirit of the chosen, working in them that unfeigned closing therewith, that makes it effectual to their undoubted salvation; which indeed is the cause that not only in other ages, but also to this day, there is a remnant that receive this grace; they being appointed, I say, thereto, before the world began; preserved in time from that which would undo them, and enabled to embrace the glorious gospel of grace, and peace, and life. 1 Ki. xix. 18. Ro. xi. 5. 1 Th. v. 9.

Now there is a great difference between the grace of election, and the grace that is wrapped up in the general tenders of the gospel; a difference, I say, and that both as to its timing, latituding, and working.

1. Touching its timing; it is before, yea long before, there was either tender of the grace wrapped up in the gospel to any, or any need of such a tender. Ep. i. 4, 5.

2. They also differ in latitude; the tenders of grace in the gospel are common and universal to all, but the extension of that of election special and peculiar to some. 'There is a remnant according to the election of grace.' Ro. xi. 5.

3. Touching the working of the grace of election; it differs much in some things from the working of the grace that is offered in the general tenders of the gospel. As is manifest in these particulars:

(1.) The grace that is offered in the general tenders of the gospel, calleth for faith to lay hold upon, and accept thereof; but the special grace of election, worketh that faith which doth lay hold thereof. Ac. xvi. 31. xiii. 48. Phil. i. 29. 2 Th. i. 11.

(2.) The grace that is offered in the general tenders of the gospel, calleth for faith as a condition in us, without which there is no life ; but the special grace of election worketh faith in us without any such condition. Mar. xvi. 15, 16. Ro. xi. 5, 6.

(3.) The grace that is offered in the general tenders of the gospel, promiseth happiness upon the condition of persevering in the faith only; but the special grace of election causeth this perseverance. Col. i. 23. Ep. ii. 10. Ro. xi. 7. 1 Pe. i. 5—7.

(4.) The grace offered in the general tenders of the gospel, when it sparkleth most, leaveth the greatest part of men behind it; but the special grace of election, when it shineth least, doth infallibly bring every soul therein concerned to everlasting life. Ro. x. 16. viii. 33—35.

(5.) A man may overcome and put out all the light and life that is begotten in him by the general tenders of the gospel; but none shall overcome, or make void, or frustrate the grace of election. Jude 4. 2 Pe. ii. 20—22. Mat. xxiv. 24. Ro. xi. 1—3, &c.

(6.) The general tenders of the gospel, considered without a concurrence of the grace of election, helps not the elect himself, when sadly fallen. Wherefore, when I say the grace that is offered in the general tenders of the gospel, I mean that grace when offered, as not being accompanied with a special operation of God's eternal love, by way of conjunction therewith. Otherwise the grace that is tendered in the general offers of the gospel, is that which saveth the sinner now, and that brings him to everlasting life; that is, when conjoined with that grace that blesseth and maketh this general tender effectually efficacious. The grace of election worketh not without, but by these tenders generally; neither doth the grace thus tendered, effectually work, but by and with the grace of election: 'As many as were ordained to eternal life believed:' Ac. xiii. 48. The word being then effectual to life, when the hand of the Lord is effectually therewith to that end. Mar. xvi. 20. They 'spake (saith the text) unto the Grecians, preaching the Lord Jesus. And the hand of the Lord was with them; and a great number believed, and turned unto the Lord.' Ac. xi. 20, 21.

We must always put difference between the word of the gospel, and the power that manageth that word; we must put difference between the common and more special operations of that power also; even as there is evidently a difference to be put between those words of Christ that were effectual to do what was said, and of those words of his which were but words only, or at least not so accompanied with power. As for instance: that same Jesus that said to the Leper, 'Say nothing to any man,' said also to Lazarus, 'Come forth;' yet the one obeyed, the other did not; though he that obeyed was least in a capacity to do it, he being now dead, and stunk in his grave. Indeed unbelief hath hindered Christ much, yet not when he putteth forth himself as Almighty, but when he doth suffer himself by them to be abused who are to be dealt with by ordinary means: Otherwise legions of devils, with ten thousand impediments, must fall down before him, and give way unto him. There is a speaking, and a so speaking: 'They so spake, that a great multitude, both of the Jews, and also of the Greeks, believed.' Ac xiv. 1. Even as I have hinted already, there is a difference between the coming of the word when it is in power, 1 Th. i. 5. and when it is in word only. So then, the blessed grace of election chooseth this man to good, not because he is good; it chooseth him to believe, not because he doth believe; it chooseth him to persevere, not because he doth so: it fore-ordains that this man shall be created in Christ Jesus unto good works, Ep. i. 4—6. not if a man will create himself thereto. 1 Pe. i. 2. Ep. ii. 10.

What shall we say then?   Is the fault in God, if any perish?   Doubtless no; nor yet in his act of eternal reprobation neither: it is grace that saveth the elect, but sin that damns the rest: it is superabundant grace that causeth the elect to close with the tenders of life, and live; and it is the aboundings of sin that holds off the reprobate from the rational, necessary, and absolute tenders, of grace.   To conclude then; the gospel calleth for credence as a condition, and that both from the elect and. reprobate; but because none of them both, as dead in sin, will close therewith, and live; therefore grace, by virtue of electing love, puts forth itself to work and do for some beyond reason; and justice cuts off others, for slighting so good, so gracious, and necessary a means of salvation, so full both of kindness, mercy and reason.

Seeing [that] *it is not possible that the reprobate should receive this grace and live, and also seeing* [that] *this is infallibly foreseen of God; and again, seeing God hath fore-determined to suffer it so to be; Why doth he yet will and command that the gospel, and so grace in the general tenders thereof, should be proffered unto them?*

Why then is the gospel offered them? Well, that there is such a thing as eternal reprobation, I have shewed you; also what this eternal reprobation is, I have opened unto you: and shall now shew you also, that though these reprobates will infallibly perish, which God not only foresaw, but fore-determined to suffer them most assuredly so to do; yet there is reason, great reason, why the gospel, and so the grace of God thereby, should be tendered, and that in general terms, to them as well as others.

But before I come to lay the reasons before you, I must mind you afresh of these particulars:

1. That eternal reprobation makes no man a sinner.

2. That the fore-knowledge of God that the reprobate would perish makes no man a sinner.

3. That God's infallibly determining upon the damnation of him that perisheth, makes no man a sinner.

4. God's patience and long-suffering, and forbearance, until the reprobate fits himself for eternal destruction, makes no man a sinner.

So then, God may reprobate, may suffer the
reprobate to sin, may fore-determine his infallible
damnation, through the pre-consideration of him in
sin, and may also forbear to work that effectual
work in his soul that would infallibly bring him
out of this condition, and yet neither be the au-
author, contriver, nor means of man's sin and
misery.

Again, God may infallibly foresee that this reprobate, when he hath sinned, will be an unreasonable opposer of his own salvation; and may
also determine to suffer him to sin, and be thus
unreasonable to the end, yet be gracious, yea very
gracious, if he offer him life, and that only upon
reasonable terms, which yet he denieth to close
with. Is. i. 18. lv. 12.

The reasons are,

1. Because not God, but sin, hath made him
unreasonable; without which, reasonable terms
had done his work for him: for reasonable terms
are the most equal and righteous terms that can
be propounded between parties at difference; yea
the terms that most suiteth and agreeth with a
reasonable creature, such as man; nay, reasonable
terms are, for terms, the most apt to work with
that man whose reason is brought into and held
captive by very sense itself. Eze. xviii.; xxxiii.

2. God goeth yet further, he addeth promises
of mercy, as those that are inseparable to the
terms he offereth, even to pour forth his Spirit
unto them; 'Turn at my reproof, and behold I
will pour forth of my Spirit unto you, and incline
your ear; come unto me, hear and your soul shall
live.' Pr. i. 23—27.

Now then to the question itself, to wit, that seeing it is impossible the reprobate should be saved; seeing also this is infallibly foreseen of God, and seeing also that God hath beforehand determined to suffer it so to be; yet I shall shew you it is requisite, yea very requisite, that he should both will and command that the gospel, and so grace in the general tenders thereof should be proffered unto them.

First Reason.—And that first, to shew that this reprobation doth not in itself make any man absolutely incapable of salvation: for if God had intended that by the act of reprobation, the persons therein concerned should also by that only act have been made incapable of everlasting life, then this act must also have tied up all the means from them, that tendeth to that end; or at least have debarred the gospel's being offered to them by God's command, for that intent; otherwise who is there but would have charged the Holy One as guilty of guile, and worthy of blame, for commanding that the gospel of grace and salvation should be offered unto this or that man, whom yet he hath made incapable to receive it, by his act of reprobation. Wherefore this very thing, to wit, that the gospel is yet to be tendered to those eternally reprobated, sheweth that it is not simply the act of God's reprobation, but sin, that incapacitateth the creature of live everlasting. Which sin is no branch of this reprobation, as is evident, because the elect and reprobate are both alike defiled therewith.

Second Reason.—God also sheweth by this, that the reprobate do not perish for want of the offers of salvation, though he hath offended God, and that upon most righteous terms; according to what is written, 'As I live, saith the Lord God, I have no pleasure in the death of the wicked, but that the wicked turn from his way, and live.' Eze. xxxiii. 11; xviii. 31, 32. 'Turn ye unto me, saith the Lord of Hosts, and I will turn unto you, saith the Lord of Hosts.' Zec. i. 3. So then, here lieth the point between God and the reprobate, I mean the reprobate since he hath sinned, God is willing to save him upon reasonable terms, but not upon terms above reason; but no reasonable terms will [go] down with the reprobate, therefore he must perish for his unreasonableness.

That God is willing to save even those that perish for ever, is apparent, both from the consideration of the goodness of his nature, Ps. cxlv. 9. of man's being his creature, and indeed in a miserable state. Job xiv. 15; iii. 16. But I say, as I have also said already, there is a great difference between his being willing to save them, through their complying with these his reasonable terms, and his being resolved to save them, whether they, as men, will close therewith, or no; so only he saveth the elect themselves, even 'according to the riches of his grace.' Ep. i. 7. Even 'according to his riches in glory, by Christ Jesus.' Phi. iv. 19. Working effectually in them, what the gospel, as a condition, calleth for from them. And hence it is that he is said to give faith, Phi. i. 29. yea the most holy faith, for that is the faith of God's elect, to give repentance, Ac. v. 31. to give a new heart, to give his fear, even that fear that may keep them for ever from everlasting ruin; Ep. i. 4. still engaging his mercy and goodness to follow them all the days of their lives, Je. xxxii. 40. Eze. xxxvi. 26, 27. that they may dwell in the house of the Lord for ever, Ps. xxiii. 6. and as another scripture saith, 'Now he that hath wrought us for the selfsame thing, *is* God.' 2 Co. v. 5. Ro. viii. 26, &c.

But I say, his denying to do thus for every man in the world, cannot properly be said to be because he is not heartily willing they should close with the tenders of the grace held forth in the gospel, and live. Wherefore you must consider that there is a distinction to be put between God's denying grace on reasonable terms, and denying it absolutely; and also that there is a difference between his withholding further grace, and of hindering men from closing with the grace at present offered; also that God may withhold much, when he taketh away nothing; yea, take away much, when once abused, and yet be just and righteous still. Further, God may deny to do this or that absolutely, when yet he hath promised to do, not only that, but more, conditionally. Which things considered, you may with ease conclude, that he may be willing to save those not elect, upon reasonable terms, though not without them.

It is no unrighteousness in God to offer grace unto the world, though but on these terms only, that they are also foreseen by him infallibly to reject; both because to reject it is unreasonable, especially the terms being so reasonable, as to believe the truth and live; and also because it is grace and mercy in God, so much as once to offer means of reconciliation to a sinner, he being the offender; but the Lord, the God offended; they being but dust and ashes, he the heavenly Majesty. If God, when man had broke the law, had yet with all severity kept the world to the utmost condition of it, had he then been unjust? Had he injured man at all? Was not every tittle of the law reasonable, both in the first and second table? How much more then is he merciful and gracious, even in but mentioning terms of reconciliation? especially seeing he is also willing so to condescend, if they will believe his word, and receive the love of the truth. Though the reprobate then doth voluntarily, and against all strength of reason, run himself upon the rocks of eternal misery, and split himself thereon, he perisheth in his own corruption, by rejecting terms of life. 2 Th. ii. 10. 2 Pe. ii. 12, 13.

Object. But the reprobate is not now in a capacity to fulfil these reasonable terms.

Ans. But I say, suppose it should be granted, is it because reprobation made him incapable, or sin? Not reprobation, but sin: if sin, then before he quarrel, let him consider the case aright, where, in the result, he will find sin, being consented to by his voluntary mind, hath thus disabled him: and because, I say, it was sin by his voluntary consent that did it, let him quarrel with himself for consenting, so as to make himself incapable to close with reasonable terms; yea, with those terms because reasonable, therefore most suitable, as terms, for him notwithstanding his wickedness. And I say again, forasmuch as those reasonable terms have annexed unto them, as their inseparable companions, such wonderful mercy and grace as indeed there is, let even them that perish, yet justify God; yea cry, ' His goodness endureth for ever ;' though they, through the wretchedness of their hearts, get no benefit by it.

THIRD REASON.—God may will and command that his gospel, and so the grace thereof, be ten‧dered to those that shall never be saved, (besides what hath been said) to shew to all spectators what an enemy sin, being once embraced, is to the salvation of man. Sin, without the tenders of the grace of the gospel, could never have appeared so exceeding sinful, as by that it both hath and doth: 'If I had not come and spoken unto them, (saith Christ) they had not had sin: but now they have no cloke for their sin.' Jn. xv. 22. As sins that oppose the law, are discovered by the law, that is, by the goodness, and justness, and holiness of the law; Ro. vii. so the sins that oppose the gospel, are made manifest by that, even by the love, and mercy, and forgiveness of the gospel: If 'he that despised Moses' law died without mercy, - of how much sorer punishment, suppose ye, shall he be thought worthy, who hath trodden under foot the Son of God ?' He. x. 28, 29. Who could have thought that sin would have opposed that which is just, but especially mercy and grace, had we not seen it with our eyes ? And how could we have seen it to purpose, had not God left some to themselves ? Here indeed is sin made manifest: 'For all he had done so many miracles amongst them,' (to wit, to persuade them to mercy) 'yet they believed not on him.' Jn. xii 37. Sin, where it reigneth, is a mortal ·enemy to the soul; it blinds the eyes, holds the hands, ties the legs, and stops the ears, and makes the heart implacable to resist the Saviour of souls. That man will neither obey the law nor the gospel, who is left unto his sin: which also God is willing should be discovered and made manifest, though it cost the damnation of some: For this very purpose, saith God to Pharaoh, 'have I raised thee up, for to shew *in* thee my power; and that my name may be declared in all the earth.' Ex. ix. 16. Ro. ix. 17. For God, by raising up Pharaoh to his kingdom, and suffering him to walk to the height, according as his sin did prompt him forward, shewed unto all beholders what a dreadful thing sin is; and that without the special assistance of his Holy Spirit, sin would neither be charmed by law nor gospel. This reason, though it be no profit unto those that are damned; yet it is for the honour of God, and the good of those he hath chosen.

It is for the honour of God, even for the honour of his power and mercy: for his power is now discovered indeed, when nothing can tame sin but that; and his mercy is here seen indeed; because that doth engage him to do it. Read Ro. ix. 22, 23.

Fourth Reason.—God commandeth that the tender of the gospel, and the grace thereof, be in general offered to all, that means thereby might be sufficiently provided for the elect, both to beget them to faith, and to maintain it in them to the end, in what place, or state, or condition soever they are. Ep. i. God, through the operation of his manifold wisdom, hath an end and an end in his acts and doings amongst the children of men: and, so in that he commandeth that his gospel be tendered to all, an end, I say, to leave the damned without excuse, and to provide sufficiency of means for the gathering all his elect. 'Oh that God would speak, (saith Zophar,) and open his lips against thee; and - shew thee the secrets of wisdom, that *they are* double to that which is.' Job xi. 5, 6. For though God worketh with and upon the elect, otherwise than with and upon the reprobate; yet he worketh with and upon the elect, with and by the same word he commandeth should be held forth and offered to the reprobate. Now the text thus running in most free and universal terms, the elect then hearing thereof, do through the mighty power of God close in with the tenders therein held forth, and are saved. Thus that word that was offered to the reprobate Jews, and by them most fiercely rejected, even that word became yet effectual to the chosen, and they were saved thereby. They gladly received the word, ' and as many as were ordained to eternal life believed.' Ac. xiii. 48.*

---

* As the same sun which softens the wax, hardens the clay, so it is with the preached gospel, which is to some ' the savour of death unto death, and to others the savour of life unto life,' 2 Cor. ii. 16. The gospel is ineffectual to any saving purpose respecting the reprobate; partly through pride, and in not enduring to-be reproved by it; partly through slothfulness, in not coming under the sound of it; and principally through cursed infidelity, in not believing the gracious message it brings. Let it be well attended to, that all who hear the gospel, are obliged to the duty of believing, as well as to all the duties of the moral law, and that before they know their particular election; for we cannot have a certain knowledge of our election to eternal life before we do believe: it is a thing hidden in the unsearchable counsel of God, until it be manifest by our effectual calling, and believing on Christ; therefore we must believe on Christ before we know our election; or else we shall never know it, and shall never believe. All joy, peace, comfort, assurances, are communicated to the soul in the way of believing. May the Lord give and increase saving faith!—*Mason and Ryland.*

'Not as though the word of God had taken none effect.' Ro. ix. 6. 'God hath not cast away his people whom he foreknew.' xi. 2. The word shall accomplish the thing for which God hath sent it, even the salvation of the few that are chosen, when tendered to all; though rejected by most, through the rebellion of their hearts. Ac. xxviii. 28. He. iv. 1—3.

Object. But if God hath elected, as you have said, what need he lay a foundation so general for the begetting faith in his chosen particulars, seeing the same Spirit that worketh in them by such means, could also work in them by other, even by a word, excluding the most, in the first tenders thereof, amongst men?

Ans. I told you before, that though this be a principal reason of the general tenders of the grace of the gospel, yet it is not all the reason why the tender should be so general, as the three former reasons shew.

But again, in the bowels of God's decree of election, is contained the means that are also ordained for the effectual bringing of those elected to that glory for which they were fore-appointed; even to gather together in one, all the children of God. Jn. xi. 52. 'Whereunto he called you, (saith Paul,) by our gospel, to the obtaining of the glory of our Lord Jesus Christ.' 2 Th. ii. 14. God's decree of election then, destroyeth not the means which his wisdom hath prepared, it rather establisheth, yea ordains and establisheth it; and maketh that means which in the outward sound is indefinite and general, effectual to this and that man, through a special and particular application: Ga. ii. 20, 21. thus *that* Christ that in general was offered to all, is by

a special act of faith applied to Paul in particular;
'He loved me, and gave himself for me.'

Further, As the design of the Heavenly Majesty
is to bring his elect to glory by means, so by the
means thus universal and general, as most behoove-
ful and fit; if we consider not only the way it doth
please him to work with some of his chosen, in
order to this their glory, but also the trials, temptations, and other calamities they must go through
thereto.

1. Touching his working with some, how invisible
is it to those in whose souls it is yet begun? How
is the word buried under the clods of their hearts
for months, yea years together?   Only thus much
is discovered thereof, it sheweth the soul its sin,
the which it doth also so aggravate and apply to
the conscience (Jesus still refraining, like Joseph,
to make himself known to his brethren) that were
there not general tenders of mercy, and that to the
worst of sinners, they would soon miscarry, and
perish, as do the sons of perdition.   But by these
the Lord upholdeth and helpeth them, that they
stand, when others fall for ever. Ps. cxix. 49.

2. And so likewise for their trials, temptations,
and other calamities, because God will not bring
them to heaven without, but by them; therefore
he hath also provided a word so large, as to lie
fair for the support of the soul in all conditions,
that it may not die for thirst.

3. I might add also in this place, their imperfect state after grace received, doth call for such
a word; yea, many other things which might be
named: which God, only wise, hath thought fit
should accompany us to the ship, yea in the sea,

to our desired haven.

Fifth Reason.—God willeth and commandeth the gospel should be offered to all, that thereby distinguishing love, as to an inward and spiritual work, might the more appear to be indeed the fruit of special and peculiar love. For in that the gospel is tendered to all in general, when yet but some do receive it; yea, and seeing these some are as unable, unwilling, and by nature, as much averse thereto, as those that refuse it, and perish; it is evident that something more of heaven and the operation of the Spirit of God doth accompany the word thus tendered for their life and salvation that enjoy it. 1 Th. i. 4—7. Not now as a word barely tendered, but backed by the strength of heaven: 'Behold what manner of love the Father hath bestowed upon us, that we should be called the sons of God!' 1 Jn. iii. 1. even we who believe 'according to the working of his mighty power, which he wrought in Christ, when he raised him from the dead.' Ep. i. 20. This provoketh to distinguishing admiration, yea, and also to a love like that which hath fastened on the called, the preserved, and the glorified: 'He hath not dealt so with any nation: and *as for his* judgments, they have not known them. Praise ye the Lord.' Ps. cxlvii. 20. Now are the sacrifices bound even to the horns of the altar, with a 'Lord, how is it that thou wilt manifest thyself unto us, and not unto the world!' Jn. xiv. 22. He 'sent from above, he took me; he drew me out of many waters; he delivered me from my strong enemy, *and* from them that hated me; for they were too strong for me.' 2 Sa. xxii. 17. Ps. xviii. 16.

For thus the elect considereth: though we all

came alike into the world, and are the children of wrath by nature; Ep. ii. 1—3. yea, though we have alike so weakened ourselves by sin, Ro. iii. 9. that the whole head is sick, and the whole heart faint, Is. i. 5. being altogether gone out of the way, and every one become altogether unprofitable, both to God and ourselves; Ro. iii. 12. yet that God should open mine eyes, convert my soul, give me faith, forgive my sins, raise me, when I fall; fetch me again, when I am gone astray; this is wonderful! Ps. xxxvii. 23. Yea, that he should prepare eternal mansions for me; Ps. xxiii. 6. and also keep me by his blessed and mighty power for that; and that in a way of believing, which without his assistance I am no way able to perform! 2 Co. v. 5. That he should do this notwithstanding my sins, though I had no righteousness! De. ix. 5—7. Yea, that he should do it according to the riches of his grace, through the redemption that is in Jesus Christ our Lord! Even according to an everlasting covenant of grace, which yet the greatest part of the world are void of, and will for ever miss and fall short of! Eze. xvi. 60—63. Besides, that he should mollify my heart! break it, and then delight in it; Ps. li. 17. put his fear in it, and then look to me, Is. lxvi. 2. Ps. cxxxviii. 6. and keep me as the apple of his eye; De. xxxii. 10. yea, resolve to guide me with his counsel, and then receive me to glory! Further, that all this should be the effect of unthought of, undeserved, and undesired love! Mal. i. 2. De. vii. 7, 8. That the Lord should think on this before he made the world, Je. xxxi. 3. and sufficiently ordain the means before he had laid the foundation of the hills! For this he is worthy to be praised: 1 Co. ii. 9. yea,

' Let every thing that hath breath praise the Lord; praise ye the Lord.'

Object. But you have said before, that the reprobate is also blessed with many gospel mercies, as with the knowledge of Christ, faith, light, the gift of the Holy Ghost, and the tastes or relish 'of the powers of the world to come: if so, then what should be the reason that yet he perisheth? Is it because the grace that he receiveth differeth from the grace that the elect are saved by? If they differ, where lieth the difference? Whether in the nature, or in the degree, or in the management thereof?

Ans. To this objection I might answer many things; but, for brevity, take this reply: That the non-elect may travel very far both in the knowledge, faith, light, and sweetness of Jesus Christ, and may also attain to the partaking of the Holy Ghost; yea, and by the very operation of these things also, escape the pollutions of the world, and become a visible saint, join in church-communion, and be as chief amongst the very elect themselves. This the scriptures every where do shew us.

The question then is, whether the elect and reprobate receive a differing grace? To which I answer, Yes, in some respects, both as to the nature thereof, and also the degree.

1. To begin then with the nature of it.

(1.) The faith that the chosen are blessed with, it goeth under another name than any faith besides, even the faith of God's elect, Tit. i. 1. as of a faith belonging to them only, of which none others do partake; which faith also, for the nature of it, is called faith most holy; Jude 20. to shew it goes

beyond all other, and can be fitly matched no
where else, but with their most blessed faith who
infallibly attain eternal glory : even 'like precious
faith with us,' saith Peter ; 2 Pe. i. 1. with his elect
companions. And so of other things. For if this
be true, that they differ in their faith, they must
needs therewith differ in other things : for faith
being the mother grace, produceth all the rest
according to its own nature, to wit, love that
abounds, that never fails, and that is never con-
tented till it attain the resurrection of the dead, &c.
2 Th. i. 3. 1 Co. xiii. 8. Phi. iii.

(2.) They differ as to the nature, in this ; the
faith, and hope, and love, that the chosen receive,
it is that which floweth from election itself ; he
hath blessed us ' according as he hath chosen us,'
Ep. i. 4, 5. even with those graces he set apart for us,
when he in eternity did appoint us to life before
the foundation of the world : which graces, because
the decree in itself is most absolute and infallible,
they also, that they may completely answer the end,
will do the work infallibly likewise, still through
the management of Christ : ' I have prayed for
thee, that thy faith fail not.' Lu. xxii. 32.   But,

2. As they differ in nature, they differ also in
degree : for though it be true that the reprobate
is blessed with grace, yet this is also as true, that
the elect are blessed with more grace. It is the
privilege only of those that are chosen, to be blessed
with ALL spiritual blessings, and to have ALL the
good pleasure of the goodness of God fulfilled in
and upon them. Those who are blessed with ALL
spiritual blessings must needs be blessed with eternal life ; and those in whom the Lord, not only

works all his good pleasure, but fulfilleth all the good pleasure of his goodness upon them, they must needs be preserved to his heavenly kingdom; Ep. i. 4, 5. 1 Th. i. 10. but none of the non-elect have these things conferred upon them ; therefore the grace bestowed upon the one, doth differ both in nature and degree from the other.

3. There is a difference as to the management also. The reprobate is principal for the management of the grace he receiveth, but Jesus Christ is principal for the management of the grace the elect receiveth. When I say principal, I mean chief ; for though the reprobate is to have the greatest hand in the management of what mercy and goodness the Lord bestoweth on him, yet not so as that the Lord will not help him at all ; nay contrariwise he will, if first the reprobate do truly the duty that lieth on him: 'If thou doest well, shalt thou not be accepted ? but if thou doest not well, sin lieth at the door.' Ge. iv. 7. Thus it was also with Saul, who was rejected of God upon this account. 1 Sa. xiii. 11—14; xv. 26. And I say, as to the elect themselves, though Jesus Christ our blessed Saviour be chief, as to the management of the grace bestowed on his chosen, yet not so as that he quite excludeth them from ' striving according to his working, which worketh in me mightily.' Col. i. 29. Nay contrariwise, if those who in truth are elect, shall yet be remiss, and do wickedly, they shall feel the stroke of God's rod, it may be till their bones do break. But because the work doth not lie at their door to manage as chief, but as Christ's, therefore though he may perform his work with much bitterness and grief to them ; yet

he being engaged as the principal, will perform that which concerneth them, even until the day (the coming) of Jesus Christ. Ps. cxxxviii. 8. Phi. i. 6.

From what hath been said, there ariseth this conclusion:

The elect are always under eternal mercy, but those not elect always under eternal justice; for you must consider this: there is eternal mercy and eternal justice, and there is present mercy and present justice. So then, for a man to be in a state of mercy, it may be either a state of mercy present, or both present and eternal also. And so again for a man to be in a state under justice, it may be understood either of present justice only, or of both present and eternal also.

That this may yet further be opened, I shall somewhat enlarge.

I begin with present mercy and present justice. That which I call present mercy, is that faith, light, knowledge, and taste of the good word of God, that a man may have, and perish. This is called in scripture, Believing for a while, during for a while, and rejoicing in the light for a season. He. vi. 4, 5. 2 Pe. ii. 20. Mat. xiii. 22. Lu. viii. 13. Now I call this mercy, both because none, as men, can deserve it, and also because the proper end thereof is to do good to those that have it. But I call it present mercy, because those that are only blessed with that, may sin it away, and perish ; as did some of the Galatians, Hebrews, Alexandrians, with the Asians, and others. Ga. v. 4. He. xii. 15, 16. 1 Ti. i. 20. 2 Ti. ii. 18; i. 15. He. xii. 15. But yet observe again, I do not call this present mercy, because God hath determined it shall last but a while absolutely; but because it is possible for man to lose it, yea determined he shal!, conditionally. Jn. v. 35. 1 Co. xii. 7.

Again, as to present justice, it is that which lasteth but a while also; and as present mercy is properly the portion of those left out of God's election, so present justice chiefly hath to do with God's beloved; who yet at that time are also under eternal mercy. This is that justice that afflicted Job, ch. vi. 4. David, Ps. lxxxviii.; xxxviii. 3. Heman, and the godly, who notwithstanding do infallibly attain, by virtue of this mercy, eternal life and glory. Am. iii. 2. 1 Co xi. 30, 31. Ps. xxx. 5; ciii. 9. 1 Pe. i. 6. I call this justice, because in some sense God dealeth with his children according to the quality of their transgressions; and I call it also present justice, because though the hand of God for the present be never so heavy on those that are his by election, yet it lasteth but a while; wherefore though this indeed be called wrath, yet is but a little wrath, wrath for a moment, time, or season. ' In a little wrath I hid my face from thee for a moment; but with everlasting kindness will I have mercy on thee, saith the LORD thy Redeemer.' Is. liv. 8.

Thus you see there is present mercy and present justice; also that the elect may be under present justice, when the rest may be under present mercy.

Again, As there is present mercy and present justice, so there is eternal mercy and eternal justice: and I say, as the elect may be under present justice, when the non-elect may be under present mercy; so the elect at that time are also under eternal mercy, but the other under eternal justice.

That the elect are under eternal mercy, and

that when under present justice, is evident from what hath been said before, namely, from their being chosen in Christ before the foundation of the world; as also from the consideration of their sound conversion, and safe preservation quite through this wicked world, even safe unto eternal life; as he also saith by the prophet Jeremiah, 'Yea, I have loved thee with an everlasting love: therefore with loving kindness have I drawn thee.' ch. xxxi. 3.   And hence it is that he calleth the elect his sheep, Jn. x. 16. his children, xi. 52. and people, Ac. xviii. 9, 10. and that before conversion; for though none of them as yet were his children by calling, yet were they his according to election.

Now the elect being under this eternal grace and mercy, they must needs be under it both before present justice seizeth upon them, while it seizeth them, and also continueth with them longer than present justice can, it being from everlasting to everlasting.   This being so, here is the reason why no sin, nor yet temptation of the enemy, with any other evil, can hurt or destroy those thus elect of God: yea this is that which maketh even those things that in themselves are the very bane of men, yet prove very much for good to those within this purpose; Ro. viii. 28. And as David saith, '*It is* good for me that I have been afflicted.' Ps. cxix. 71. And again, 'But when we are judged we are chastened of the Lord, that we should not be condemned with the world.' 1 Co. xi. 32.   Now afflictions, · &c., in themselves are not only fruitless and unprofitable, but, being unsanctified, are destructive; 'I smote him, and he went on frowardly:' Is. lvii. 17.   But now eternal mercy working with this or that affliction, makes it profitable to the chosen; 'I have seen his ways, and will heal him, and restore comforts unto him and to his mourners.' ver. 18.   As he saith in another place, 'Blessed *is* the man whom thou chastenest, and teachest him out of thy law.' Ps. xciv. 12.   For eternal mercy doth not look on those who are the elect and chosen of God, as poor sinful creatures only, but also as the generation whom the Lord hath blessed, in whom he hath designed to magnify his mercy to the utmost, by pardoning the transgressions of the remnant of his heritage. 1 Pe. ii. 9. Mi. vii. 18, 19.   'Having predestinated us unto the adoption of children by Jesus Christ to himself, - wherein he hath made us accepted in the beloved.' Ep. i. 6.   Wherefore, I say, the elect, as they do also receive that grace and mercy that may be sinned away, so they have that grace and mercy which cannot be lost, and that sin cannot deprive them of, even mercy that abounds, and goeth beyond all sin; such mercy as hath engaged the power of God, the intercession of Christ, and the communication of the blessed Spirit of adoption, which Spirit also engageth the heart, directs it into the love of God, that it may not depart from God after that rate as the reprobates do. Ep. v. 29, 30.   'I will make an everlasting covenant with them, (saith God) that I will not turn away from them, to do them good; but I will put my fear in their hearts, that they shall not depart from me.' Je. xxxii. 40.

But now I say, God's dealing with the non-elect, is far otherwise, they being under the consideration of eternal justice, even then when in the enjoyment of present grace and mercy.   And hence it is that as to their standing before the God of heaven, they are counted dogs, and sows, and devils, even then when before the elect of God themselves they are counted saints and brethren: 'The dog *is* turned to his own vomit again, and the sow that was washed to her wallowing in the mire.' 2 Pe. ii. 22.　And the reason is, because notwithstanding all their shew before the world, their old nature and corruptions do still bear sway within, which in time also, according to the ordinary judgment of God, is suffered so to shew itself, that they are visible to saints that are elect, as was the case of Simon Magus, and that wicked apostate Judas, who 'went out from us, but they were not of us; for if they had been of us, they would *no doubt* have continued with us : but *they went out* that they might be made manifest that they were not all of us:' 1 Jn. ii. 19.　They were not elect as we, nor were they sanctified as the elect of God themselves ; wherefore eternal justice counts them the sons of perdition, when under their profession.　And I say, they being under this eternal justice, it must needs have to do with them in the midst of their profession; and because also it is much offended with them for conniving with their lust, it taketh away from them, and that most righteously, those gifts and graces, and benefits and privileges that present mercy gave them ; and not only so, but cuts them off for their iniquity, and layeth them under wrath for ever. They 'have forsaken the right way, (saith God) - following the way of Baalam *the son* of Bosor ; - these are wells without water, clouds that are carried with a tempest;' trees whose fruit withereth, without fruit, twice dead, plucked up by the roots,

' for whom is reserved the blackness of darkness for ever.' 2 Pe. ii. 5, 16, 17. Jude 11—13. Jn. xvii. 12. Mat. xiii. 12; xxv. 29. Mar. iv. 25. Lu. viii. 18.

These things thus considered, you see,

1. That there is present grace and present mercy, eternal grace and eternal mercy.

2. That the elect are under eternal mercy, and THAT, when under present justice; and that the reprobate is under eternal justice, and THAT when under present mercy.

3. Thus you see again, that the non-elect perish by reason of sin, notwithstanding present mercy, because of eternal justice; and that the elect are preserved from the death, though they sin and are obnoxious to the strokes of present justice, by reason of eternal mercy. What shall we say then? Is there unrighteousness with God? God forbid: 'He hath mercy on whom he will have mercy, and compassion on whom he will have compassion.' Ro. ix. 15.